The Perfect Kingdom?

(Full Colour)

22 Studies in 1 & 2 Chronicles

by David W. Legg

Covenant Books UK

COVENANT BOOKS UK (CBUK)
10 Kelsey Close, Liss. GU33 7HR
Email: office@covenantbooksuk.org.uk
Website: https://covenantbooksuk.org.uk/
© David W. Legg 2024

First published by *Covenant Books UK* in 2024.

David W. Legg has asserted his right under the Copyright, Designs and Patents Act, 1988, UK, to be identified as author of this work. All rights reserved. No part of this publication may be reproduced, stored in a retrieval system or transmitted in any form or by any means, electronic, mechanical, photocopying, recording or otherwise, without prior permission of the authors or other copyright holders. Covenant Books UK has been granted exclusive rights to publish this work. Covenant Books UK does not necessarily endorse all the views presented herein, but considers the overall work valuable.

ESV: Except where noted, scripture quotations are from the ESV® Bible (The Holy Bible, English Standard Version®, Anglicised, copyright © 2001 by Crossway, a publishing ministry of Good News Publishers. Used by permission. All rights reserved.

NIV: Where noted, scripture quotations are taken from The Holy Bible, New International Version (Anglicised Edition) Copyright © 1973, 1978, 1984, 2011 by Biblica (formerly International Bible Society). Used by permission of Hodder & Stoughton Publishers, a Hachette UK company. All rights reserved worldwide. NIV® UK Trademark number 1448790.

Note that occasionally, residual American spellings etc. have been corrected to English.

Photographs and diagrams are all owned by the author, except where otherwise indicated, or are in the public domain or whose use constitutes fair use under US law. Photographs from *Wikipedia* and/or *Wikimedia Commons* (https://commons.wikimedia.org/) are used under the *Creative Commons Attribution-Share Alike Unported* licence, CC BY-SA version 2.5 or higher, *Gnu* or *FDL*, or are in the public domain, unless otherwise stated.

Created in *LibreOffice Community* 7.6.4.1 with open source software on *Fedora*™ *39 Linux*™.

Colour Paperback ISBN: 9798880359301

A manual of Bible studies covering the whole book of Chronicles, for use by small groups or individuals.

The first kingdom of God on earth models for us the perfect final kingdom of God on the new earth brought about by King Jesus himself. Both positive and negative lessons are drawn and theology extracted from Chronicles in such a way as to benefit the modern reader or small group exploring the Bible together.

By means of carefully set instructions, questions, discussions, tables, maps, photographs and other helpful material, readers are enabled to cover the whole book in just 22 studies, whilst reading the majority of the biblical text. These notes bring the study of Chronicles within easy reach of a group that meets weekly.

The notes compare and contrast the "Chronicler's" approach with that of other biblical authors. He is compiling a spiritual history of the nation for the benefit of the exiles who have returned to Jerusalem. But, the lessons he highlights are very relevant to 21st Century Christians who are endeavouring to put first the kingdom of God nowadays.

The small group leader with pressing time commitments will readily be able to lead enjoyable and applied Bible studies that cover all of the book of Chronicles.

David Legg ministered in Devon (UK), and now lives and writes in Hampshire. He is married to Sue; they are members of Trinity Church Liphook, have three sons, a daughter-in-law and a grandson. His other books published by Covenant Books UK include:

- *Covenants for Evangelicals*
- *Humour in the Bible?*
- *The Right End of the Stick*
- *Reformed Evangelical Ministry Resources*
- *Local Church Membership*

See also these discussion Bible Study guides for small groups and individual use:
- *The Genesis Roller-coaster,*
- *The Exodus Experiment,*
- *1 and 2 Samuel,*
- *The Songs of Ascents and Eight Last Davidic Psalms (Psalms 120 to 145) and*
- *Ephesians.*

Please see the table of **Contents** starting on page 5.

Please check the **General Index** (page 117) for subjects without obvious headings in the above table of contents.

The **Scripture Index** (page 121) allows you to work backwards from Bible texts to their use in this manual.

Contents

1 Introduction 7
   1.1 Historical background to Chronicles 7
   1.2 Chronicles: Redressing the balance 10

2 The identity of the perfect kingdom 13
   Study 1 ■ 1 Chronicles 1-9:34 – Just a boring list? 13

3 The kings of the perfect kingdom 17
   Study 2 ■ 1 Chronicles 9:35-12:40 – David's perfect reign begins? 19
   Study 3 ■ 1 Chronicles 13-16 – Serving the perfect God 23
   Study 4 ■ 1 Chronicles 16 – Thankful but divided worship 27
   Study 5 ■ 1 Chronicles 17 – The promised everlasting king 31
   Study 6 ■ 1 Chronicles 18-20 – The victory of the messianic king 35
   Study 7 ■ 1 Chronicles 21:1–22:1 – A mystery and the heart of the gospel 39
   Study 8 ■ 1 Chronicles 22:1-19 – Solomon king of peace 43
   Study 9 ■ 1 Chronicles 23-27 – Levites and the priesthood of all believers 47
   Study 10 ■ 1 Chronicles 28-29 – David's and Solomon's hearts 51
   Study 11 ■ 2 Chronicles 1-2 – Solomon seeks God's kingdom (at) first 55
   Study 12 ■ 2 Chronicles 3-6 – The perfect house of God 59
   Study 13 ■ 2 Chronicles 7-9 – Solomon, the perfect king? 63

4 The division of the perfect kingdom 67
   Study 14 ■ 2 Chronicles 10-12 – Imperfect King Rehoboam 69
   Study 15 ■ 2 Chronicles 13-16 – *The Lord is with you while you are with him* ... 73
   Study 16 ■ 2 Chronicles 17-21:3 – Jehoshaphat models repentance 77
   Study 17 ■ 2 Chronicles 21:4-24:27 – Families! 81
   Study 18 ■ 2 Chronicles 25-28 – How good is your king? 85

5 The continuation of the perfect kingdom? 91
   Study 19 ■ 2 Chronicles 29-32 – Hezekiah, a truly Christlike king 93
   Study 20 ■ 2 Chronicles 33 – Manasseh: Amazing Grace! 97
   Study 21 ■ 2 Chronicles 34-35 – Josiah delays disaster 103
   Study 22 ■ 2 Chronicles 36:1-23 – The end of the perfect kingdom? 107

6 Whatever happened to the perfect kingdom? 113

Appendix A – The Hebrew Bible (Tanak) 115

General Index 117

Scripture Index 121

1 Introduction

1.1 Historical background to Chronicles

Chronicles was originally a single book of the Bible, probably written by Ezra, but let us call the writer 'the Chronicler' because of the measure of uncertainty that surrounds its authorship.

This largest 'book' in the Hebrew Bible[1], after the Psalms, was divided into the two parts we know today when the Hebrew Old Testament (OT) was translated into Greek[2]. In Greek, Chronicles took up more room on a scroll than in Hebrew[3], so two scrolls were required rather than the original one. We now call these '1 and 2 Chronicles', or 'First and Second Chronicles', but they should always be thought of as a single book of the Bible. They share the same context, background, purpose, concerns and author, hence the single gold[4] column running down the table on page Error: Reference source not found. The table shows how Chronicles overlaps with other biblical books. It also shows which kings, prophets and major events are covered.

The Chronicler starts remarkably simply with Adam, and traces how God's Jewish people came about by means of detailed genealogical lists. He then focusses on the kings and prophets of Israel, the division of the kingdom into two parts – the northern kingdom (known, confusingly, as Israel) and the southern one (known as Judah). The northern kingdom descends into idolatry and is exiled (722 BC). Later, the southern kingdom follows a similar path and is taken into exile in Babylon[58] (586 BC). After about 70 years[5], a new Medo-Persian emperor, Cyrus, decrees that the exiled tribes should return and rebuild God's temple in Jerusalem, in March 538 BC.

---

1   See Appendix A – The Hebrew Bible (Tanak) on page 115. The book of 'Psalms' is divided into five sub-books.
2   In around 250 BC, as part of the 'Old Greek' *Septuagint* (LXX). See *An Evangelical Appeal for the Septuagint*, C.W. Henry, *Covenant Books UK*, 2021: https://www.amazon.co.uk/dp/B09FC6DZ35
3   Mainly because the original Paleo-Hebrew, later Hebrew and Aramaic were written without any vowels, making them more compact. The division of Samuel and Kings are two more examples of this purely practical measure.
4   Or grey if you are reading this on a black & white Kindle or on paper.
5   Perhaps counting from when the very first deportations happened in 607/8 BC. Jeremiah prophesied that the exile would end after 70 years in Jeremiah 25:12; 29:10.

KING	PROPHET	ABOUT	CHRONICLES	SAMUEL/KINGS
Saul	Various	Genealogies – Adam to King Saul; Death of Saul (1010 BC)	1 Chronicles 1:1–9:44; 10:1–14	1 Samuel 31:1–2 Samuel 1:16
Saul David	Samuel Nathan Gad	David king of Judah; David king over all Israel. David's preparation for the temple	1 Chronicles 11:1–29:20	2 Samuel 1:17–24:1–25
David Solomon	Nathan	Solomon's coronation; Death of David (970 BC)	1 Chronicles 29:21–29:30	1 Kings 1:1–2:46
Solomon, Rehoboam, Jeroboam I (Israel), Rehoboam (Judah), Abijah (Judah), Asa (Judah), Ahab (Israel), Jehoshaphat (Judah), Ahaziah (Israel)	Elijah Elisha Micaiah	Solomon asks for wisdom; ... Building the temple ... Solomon's apostasy and chastisement; death (930 BC) ... Division of the kingdom; - Jeroboam I (Israel); - Rehoboam (Judah); War between Judah and Israel;	2 Chronicles 1:1–21:3	1 Kings 3:1-22:53
J(eh)oram (Judah) ... Pekah (Israel) Jotham (Judah only from here on) Ahaz Hezekiah, Manasseh, Amon, Josiah Jehoahaz, Jehoiakim, Zedekiah, Jehoiachin	Elisha Jonah Isaiah Jeremiah	... Fall of Israel and explanation (722 BC); ... Babylonian[58] captivity (~70 years[5]); Fall of Jerusalem (586 BC); Remnant flees to Egypt (586 BC)	2 Chronicles 21:4–36:21	2 Kings 1:1-25:30
Cyrus	Various	Proclamation by the Medo-Persian Emperor Cyrus (538 BC)	2 Chronicles 36:22–23	Ezra 1:1-4
	Ezra?	Chronicles written (450 BC (±63 years)[7])		

How Chronicles fits in

The table above shows how Chronicles mainly covers the same historical period as the books of Samuel and Kings. This considerable overlap rather begs the question,

'Why bother studying Chronicles if it is the same history as in Samuel and Kings?'[6]

---

[6] The early genealogies in 1 Chronicles 1 and the small overlap with Ezra are not covered in Samuel or Kings.

Chronicles covers both the same and different material, with a different focus, another purpose, and it was written much later in time to a very different readership.

Samuel was written after the death of king Solomon in 930 BC, and concerns the need for a godly shepherd king whose heart is in tune with the LORD's (1 Samuel 16:7).

Kings was written some time after the fall of Jerusalem 586 BC, to explain how Israel's covenant unfaithfulness, mainly idolatry, resulted in:

a) the exile of first the northern kingdom (2 Kings 17), then,

b) the exile of the southern kingdom to Babylon (2 Kings 25:11), and finally,

c) the flight of the remaining occupants of Jerusalem to Egypt (2 Kings 25:26).

The Chronicler uses material from both Samuel and Kings, but there the similarities end, because:

1. He wrote at a much later date, 450 BC (±63 years)[7].

2. He wrote after the *return* from the Babylonian and other exiles.

3. He makes important omissions and additions in order to draw different lessons.

4. He wrote to a people who had received God's curses in Deuteronomy 28:15-68 and Leviticus 18:28,

    '... if you defile the land, it will vomit you out as it vomited out the nations that were before you' (NIV),

    who were living among the pagans for 70 or more years, away from their land, tribes, kings, law, temple and sacrifices.

5. He wrote to a people who may have been confused about their national, linguistic[8] and spiritual identity. They were worried about whether God was really with them or not, and discouraged by the possibility that the destruction of Jerusalem and its temple might really have been the end of the kingdom of God and any hope of the Messiah ever coming to save them.

That final concern should resonate with the feelings of 21st century Christians too (Hebrews 10:25), showing the vital relevance of Chronicles to us in the here and now.

So, it is important when reading Chronicles to think:

---

7 See *1 and 2 Chronicles*, Richard L. Pratt, Mentor, CF, 1998 for how this is derived.
8 Indeed, the people came back from exile speaking Aramaic, struggling to read Hebrew (Nehemiah 8:8 and footnote in ESV and NIV).

a) Why is the Chronicler rehearsing the history of the original kings and kingdom, e.g. David etc. from 1000 BC to 586 BC?

b) How is the Chronicler making his material relevant to the returned exiles in 450 BC (±63 years)?

c) How is it relevant to modern Christians and God's kingdom nowadays?

1.2 Chronicles: Redressing the balance

Not wishing to cite specific, deathly, modernistic examples of what passed as 'scholarship' in the 19th and 20th centuries[9], we should nevertheless note in passing that some have dared to go into print asserting that Jerusalem was nothing more than a 'fortified village' in the 5th century BC, and so Chronicles was composed in order to 'create a past history' for its post-exilic denizens, thereby 'supplying a missing identity' complete with 'idealised' heroes such as a whitewashed King David and squeaky-clean Solomon!

Such claims are so annoying, that conservative evangelicals might be in danger of overreacting angrily and, thereby, not seeing the importance and sheer interest-value of what the Chronicler *omits from* his account and *adds to it*, compared with what the authors of Samuel and Kings included and excluded. It should also be said that the Chronicler's accounts of both David and Solomon are far from being hagiographies[10] (e.g. 1 Chronicles 2:3-4; 5:1; 14:3 21:8; 22:8), but they do redress the balance.

If Samuel highlights the heart problems of Saul, David and Solomon, and if Kings emphasises all the sinful reasons for Israel going into exile, then Chronicles emphasises how great and godly David and Solomon were for most of their reigns.

If the returned exiles recalled too readily David's adultery and the death of Uzzah that led to David actually being angry with the LORD (2 Samuel 6:8), if they were discouraged by Solomon's excesses in the pursuit of wisdom (1 Kings 11:3) and his eventual descent into idolatry, then they needed to recharge their sense of divine, kingly, heritage and remember that:

1 Chronicles 29:25 ... the LORD made Solomon very great in the sight of all Israel and bestowed on him such royal majesty as had not been on any king before him in Israel,

and that:

---

9   See Dale Ralph Davis' enjoyably derisive preface to *The Word Became Fresh*, Mentor, CF, 2006.
10 Idealised biographies of 'saints'.

2 Chronicles 9:22 ... King Solomon excelled all the kings of the earth in riches and in wisdom. ²³ And all the kings of the earth sought the presence of Solomon to hear his wisdom, which God had put into his mind,

and more broadly, *the LORD* saying to King David:

1 Chronicles 17:8 ... I have been with you wherever you have gone and have cut off all your enemies from before you. And I will make for you a name, like the name of the great ones of the earth. ⁹ And I will appoint a place for my people Israel and will plant them, ... and violent men shall waste them no more, as formerly, ... ¹¹ ... I will raise up your offspring after you, ... and I will establish his throne for ever.'

In addition to remembering God's blessings to them through David and Solomon they also needed to recall and believe his everlasting promise of a messiah king.

But perhaps, after their long exile in Babylon, they felt unsure of their national identity[11], discouraged by their previous failure, and confused about their current purpose in God's kingdom. Surrounded by enemies (Ezra 4:1) and beset by sin (Ezra 9:6), they urgently needed a genuine infusion of grace from the LORD. Chronicles was God's powerful, spiritual, encouragement to them; it will also strengthen us in our difficult times (2 Thessalonians 3:3).

---

11   Indeed, all through the book of Ezra they are referred to as *'the exiles'* (or similar), as if having been exiled for their national sin was now part of their actual identity.

Date	King	Prophet	Who?	1 Chronicles	Other books
>[12]1850 BC		Jacob/Israel	a *'sceptre'*		Genesis 49:10
>[12]1400 BC		Balaam	a *'sceptre'*		Numbers 24:17
>[12]1400 BC		Moses	a *king* to be allowed		Deuteronomy 17:14-17
>[12]1072 BC	Abimelech king of Shechem		*Abimelech?*		Judges 9, 2 Samuel 11:21
1375 - 1050 BC	Period of the Judges, no kings		*Perez Hezron Ram Amminadab Nahshon Boaz (m. Ruth) Obed Jesse ... (leading to King David)*	2:5-15	Ruth 4:18-22a
1050 - 1010 BC	Saul	Samuel	*Adam* to King *Saul*	**Genealogies: 1:1–9:34; 9:35-44**	Genesis 5,10, 11,35,36:31,46; 1 Samuel 8

God's kingdom prophesied and identified, but without a godly king

---

[12] I.e. Before; dates BC count backwards.

2 The identity of the perfect kingdom

Make sure you have read the introduction to these studies in chapter 1 so that all the discussion questions will have some context[13].

Study 1 ■

1 Chronicles 1-9:34 – Just a boring list?

A kingdom is surely imperfect if it has no king – see the table opposite. The first few rows show that a king was promised. Then came *Abimelech*, but he was only king of *Shechem*[14]. The 'judges' came and went; they saved from enemies, but could not make the people moral or godly (Judges 21:25).

This section of Chronicles ends with the genealogy of *Saul* (1 Chronicles 9:35-44), the first proper king. But the Chronicler is not really interested in *Saul* at this stage of his account. First, he wants to establish the spiritual and national identity of God's chosen people as a whole, as represented by the exiles who have been returning to Jerusalem since maybe 537 BC.[15](1 Chronicles 9:1-34). Only when they *re*claim their identity can they *re*occupy their land, *re*-establish their tribes, *re*member their kings, *re*cover the law of Moses, *re*build the temple, *re*-institute sacrifices, and *re*turn fully to their God.

Read 1 Chronicles 1:1-4.

Q1. Why does the Chronicler take the returned exiles all the way back to *Adam*, Genesis and creation in 1:1? (Genesis 1:1 and 50:20 may also help)

Read 1:17-28.

---

[13] Ideally, you will also be familiar with the contents of Samuel, Kings and Ezra. These books provide the background to Chronicles. The minor prophets Haggai and Zechariah also contain encouragement to the re-builders in Jerusalem.
[14] See map on page 15.
[15] With *Sheshbazzar* – see Ezra 1:8-11.

Q2. In what way does the Chronicler now narrow his focus? Why? How is this relevant to the returned exiles?

Q3. Why does the Chronicler introduce a bit of a contrast in 1:35-54?

Read 2:1-4; 5:1-2.

Q4. Why might the Chronicler make a beeline for the tribe of Judah (2:3a)? See 2:9;18 and especially 2:13-15.

Q5. What might 5:1 imply about the moral character required by leaders of God's earthly kingdom? See also 2:3; Titus 1:7.

Read 3:1-9 and 2 Chronicles 36:22-23 (538 BC).

Q6. What new, geographical, details now appear that would resonate with the newly returned exiles (3:4)?

Q7. Even at this early stage in the book, what subtle reminders are there of David's 'weaknesses' and the subsequent disasters that overtook him, his reign and his family (3:9; 2 Samuel 13:32-39)?

Q8. What other signs are there that no historical whitewashing is going on in Chronicles?

2:3	4,7[16]
3:17	5:26
6:15	

---

16   *Achar* (NIV) in 2:7 is certainly *Achan* (ESV). The modified name means 'trouble'. See Joshua 7:25.

The identity of the perfect kingdom

It is almost as if the Chronicler realises that these chapters are quite hard-going, so he incorporates little nuggets of specific encouragement into the genealogies, as follows.

Read 4:9-10.

Q9. What do we learn from *Jabez*?

Read 5:18-22.

Note that half of the tribe of *Manasseh* lived on each side of the River Jordan.

Map showing Transjordan tribes and Shechem

Q10. What do we learn from the transjordan *tribes*?

Go back and read 2:1, then 9:1-3.

Q11. How many tribes had gone into exile, and how many returned at first?[17]

How many tribes were exiled	How many returned (at first) [17]

Do the maths.

How would this make the people feel?

Application

As in 1 Chronicles 9, God's work may seem small[18] compared with the glory days of the past. But, if we are clear about our identity, our God, his people and his promises, the book of Chronicles should prove very encouraging.

No doubt, the Chronicler's detailed genealogical records helped the returning exiles to identify their place in Jewish society and worship, also to deal with the issue of who were genuine priests etc. (see Ezra 2:61-63). But, we have seen that even the most apparently 'boring' part of Chronicles is still relevant to God's modern people in 21st century.

Are we inclined to forget about God's plans, his sovereignty, that he has been in control of everything ever since before he created Adam (1:1)? Do we ever forget to include him in our own plans?

We can also forget how central to God's plans are his blood-bought people, his church-family. The Chronicler's people were right to care about returning to the geographical Jerusalem (9:3), but modern believers should transfer all that affection to the spiritual Jerusalem:

Hebrews 12:22 But you have come to Mount Zion and to the city of the living God, the heavenly Jerusalem.

In addition to being conscious of the sins of God's ancient people (9:1), we should also be humbled by our own. But we must always remember our identity as God's people in Christ, his everlasting purposes and current help through his providence, his Spirit and his word.

Do we, like Jabez (4:9), feel the pain of our circumstances and, unlike Jabez, adopt a kind of victim mentality, when we should be claiming God's promises and blessing (4:10)?

Do we try to serve God in our own strength, or do we cry out to him in the heat of battle and receive help (5:20)? Whose battle is it anyway (5:22)?

---

17   Other tribes returned too, perhaps, later. See Luke 2:36; Matthew 4:13?
18   Certainly in the UK. God's work in other parts of the world may feel more encouraging!

3 The kings of the perfect kingdom

KING	PROPHET	ABOUT	1 CHRONICLES	2 SAMUEL
Saul		Genealogy and death of King Saul	9:35-10:14	1 Samuel 31–2 Samuel 1:16
David		Lament for Saul and Jonathan		1:17–27
		David king of Judah		2:1–7
?		Ish-bosheth king over Israel		2:8–3:1
		David's sons born in Hebron; Abner defects to David		3:2–21
		Joab murders Abner; Ish-bosheth murdered		3:22–4:12
		David king over all Israel; conquers Jerusalem	11:1–9	5:1–10
		David's mighty men and the Thirty	11:10–47	23:8–39
		David's men at Ziklag; Reinforcements at Hebron	12:1–40	
		Death of Uzzah and Michal, Saul's daughter	13:1–14	6:1–11
		Michal's childlessness		6:20–23
		David's house and family in Jerusalem	14:1–7	5:11–16
		David defeats the Philistines	14:8–17	5:17–25
David		David's instructions for carrying the ark	15:1–24	
		The Ark brought to Jerusalem	15:25–16:6	6:12–19
		David's psalm of thanksgiving (Pss 105,96,106)	16:7–43	
	Nathan	Nathan's mistaken instruction to David	17:1–2	7:1–3
		Davidic covenant; David's prayer	17:3–27	7:4–29
		David's victories, officials	18:1–17	8:1–18
		David and Mephibosheth		9:1–13
		David defeats the Ammonites and Arameans (Syrians)	19:1–19	10:1–19
		Rabbah defeated in David's absence	20:1–3	11:1; 12:26–31
		David and Bathsheba		11:2–12:25
		Amnon, Tamar, and Absalom's conspiracy		13:1–14:43
		Sheba's rebellion; The Gibeonites' vengeance on Saul		20:1–21:14
		David defeats the Philistines	20:4–8	21:15–22
		David's psalm of praise (Ps 18) and last words		22:1–23:7
	Gad	David's census reveals the temple's future location	21:1–22:1	24:1–25
		David's preparation for the temple; charge to Solomon	22:2–19	
		David organises the Levites. priests, singers, gatekeepers	23:1–26:32	
	Nathan	Israel's army, officers over tribes	27:1–34	
		David's preparation for the temple; prayer of thanks	28:1–29:20	1 Kings ↓
		David and Abishag; Adonijah tries to become king		1:1–27
		Solomon's coronation	29:21–25	1:28–40
Solomon		David's instructions to Solomon		2:1–9
		Death of David	29:26–30	2:10–11
		Solomon deals with Adonijah and Joab		2:12–46
		Solomon marries Pharaoh's daughter	2 Chronicles ↓	3:1–3
		Solomon asks for wisdom to reign over Israel	1:1–13	3:4–15
		Solomon's wise judgement		3:16–28
		Solomon's wealth begins	1:14–17	4:20–34
		Solomon builds the temple	2:1–5:1	5:1–38; 7:13–51
		Solomon builds his palace	8:1b	7:1–12
		The Ark brought to the temple; The LORD's glory fills it	5:2–14	8:1–11
		Solomon blesses the people	6:1–11	8:12–21
		Solomon dedicates the temple	6:12–42	8:22–61
		Fire from the LORD consumes the sacrifices	7:1–3	
		Solomon and the people offer sacrifices	7:4–7	8:62–64
		Feast of Tabernacles	7:8–10	8:65–66
		The LORD confirms the Davidic covenant to Solomon	7:11–22	9:1–9
		Solomon's territory increases; victories	8:1–10	9:10–23
		Solomon's instructions for temple worship; his prosperity	8:11–18	9:24–28
	Ahijah, others	The Queen of Sheba visits; Solomon's splendour	9:1–28	10:1–29
		Solomon's apostasy and chastisement		11:1–40
		Solomon's death	9:29–31	11:41–43

Study 2 ■

1 Chronicles 9:35-12:40 – David's perfect reign begins?

Having noted that the Chronicler was not previously very interested in King Saul (1050-1010 BC), we should also now point out that Saul's genealogy from 8:29-38 is repeated in the same traditional style as is found in other genealogies at the ends of Genesis 11 and Ruth 4, rather than for any emphasis.

Read 1 Chronicles 10:1-14.

Q1. What clues are there that the Chronicler is not mainly interested in Saul? Count the number of verses 1 Chronicles 10. See also 10:13-14.

Having mentioned already in 3:4 that David initially ruled only in *Hebron*, over only Judah, (see the map on page 15), the Chronicler ups the pace of the account by quickly having him rule *all Israel* (11:1) and conquer Jerusalem (11:5).

Read 11:1-9.

Q2. Why might the returned exiles need to hear that David and Solomon ruled over *all Israel*?

11:1,10   18:14

29:23   2 Chronicles 9:30

See also 2 Chronicles 10:16 and John 17:20-23.

Q3. How does our Christian unity reflect upon our king (John 13:35)?

What practical effect does it have?

As a kingdom is somewhat imperfect without a king, so a king would be imperfect without some some warriors!

Read 11:10-19.

Q4. How does David react to zeal and devotion of the three mighty men (11:18-19)?

Although *the three* came back largely intact, David sees their *blood* in the *water* from *Bethlehem*.

Q5. What is God's attitude to his people who risk or even expend their lives for him? (11:18; Psalm 72:14b)?

Q6. And what should our attitude be to those who risk their lives for King Jesus?

Romans 16:3-4

Philippians 2:25,29-30

Read 12:1-2; 8-22.

Q7. At what stage of David's career was he living in *Ziklag* (12:1) or at his *stronghold in the desert* (12:8,16)? See also the explanation in 12:19 and the top of the table on page 17.

We see warriors from other tribes such as *Benjamin* (12:2), *Gad* (12:14), *Ephraim* (12:30) and *Manasseh* (12:19) joining *David*, even while Saul or his descendants were still king.

Q8. How many of the twelve tribes joined up (survey 12:23-37)? _____

The kings of the perfect kingdom

> **Q9.** Should we wait until God's kingdom is going really well before nailing our colours to the mast as Christians? Should we wait until a church is really well attended before joining as members? In short, should we be risk averse?
>
> **Discuss:**

The last verses of 1 Chronicles 12 read like a huge celebration for hundreds of thousands of people.

Read 12:38-40.

This coronation feast seems like the one in Revelation 7, just after the 12 tribes have all been sealed, remembering that Jesus is David's king of kings.

Q10. How will *the Lamb's* celebration in Revelation 7 compare with *King David's* feast in 1 Chronicles 12? Use the space for notes in the table.

1 Chronicles	Revelation 7:9-17	Notes
12:23-37 all the tribes	v9 *every nation, all tribes*	
12:38 *David king over all Israel*	v10 *the Lamb on the throne*	
12:39-40 *abundant provisions*	16 *no hunger or thirst*	
12:40 *joy in Israel*	17b *he will wipe away every tear*	
11:2 *shepherd*		

Application

It appears that David's kingdom was like Jesus' kingdom is and will be in the future, Jesus' is much better and will last for ever. Should noticing the similarities be just an intellectual exercise? Or, shouldn't we be encouraged by what we have studied, and then both pray and work in such a way that Jesus' kingdom comes here on earth now, in heaven and, one day, on the new earth for ever?

If so, we will be willing to take the risk of associating ourselves with Jesus' people here and now, even if his kingdom is struggling in some respects.

When David's men joined him at Ziklag, in the desert and in Hebron, they were taking a risk by faith. To God, there was no risk, but to those hungry men in the desert of Judah the risk was real, but they still signed up.

Meanwhile, back in the derelict city of Jerusalem, the Chronicler's people were under all sorts of pressures which, when combined with any lack of faith and their own human sin, could quickly cause the new work of God to become fragmented. Such disunity would rejoice the hearts of their enemies[19]. Disunity nowadays impairs the work of the gospel and obscures the fact that we are working for the King.

Furthermore, we have the examples of great kingdom warriors to emulate, those willing to risk their lives for the sake of King Jesus. In Philippians it was Epaphroditus. In recent centuries it was missionary heroes like John Paton[20] and social reformers like William Wilberforce[21]. Who is it at present? Whose examples (Philippians 3:17) should we be following nowadays.

---

19   These are big themes in Ezra and Nehemiah. Look out for Sanballat the Horonite, Tobiah the Ammonite and Geshem the Arab (Nehemiah 2:19).
20   See https://en.wikipedia.org/wiki/John_Gibson_Paton, accessed 2024/01/15.
21   See https://en.wikipedia.org/wiki/William_Wilberforce, accessed 2024/01/15.

Study 3 ■

1 Chronicles 13-16 – Serving the perfect God

As a genuinely spiritual king who loved God and wanted to shepherd his people wisely, David knew that he could not do it on his own as Saul before him tried to do (13:3).

Exodus 29:45 'I will dwell among the people of Israel and will be their God.'

So, David spontaneously decides to move the ark[22] of the covenant, which represented God's promised presence and blessing, into the *City of David*.

Map of Philistine territory, Kireath-Jearim and Jerusalem (The City of David)

Read 1 Chronicles 13:1-8.

22　The ark had been at Kireath-Jearim since about 1049 BC, after its return from the Philistines, and after the people of Beth-Shemeth had looked inside it and the LORD killed 70 of them (1 Samuel 6:19). *1 Chronicles*, Cyril J. Barber, CF, 2004. See map.

Q1. How does the Chronicler highlight David's ability to unite the people behind him, with good communication, maximum 'buy-in' and enthusiasm?

13:1   13:3

13:4   13:5   13:8

However, it seems that enthusiasm and unity are not sufficient to serve a holy God!

Read 13:9-14. *Perez Uzzah* v11 means outbreak against Uzzah.

Q2. Who had not been consulted before the move (Numbers 27:21) despite what David said in 13:3?

Q3. What double warning does the Chronicler retain in 13:6 from Samuel's earlier account[23] (to remind the reader that the ark is not just a box!)?

Read Numbers 4:5-6; 15; 17-20; 7:6-9.

Q4. What were the divinely appointed rules for transporting the *ark of God*?

4:5   4:6

4:15

4:20   7:9

Q5. What important reason was given for the strictness of these rules?

Numbers 4:18-19a

Now read 1 Chronicles 13:7-10.

---
[23] 2 Samuel 6:2

Q6. How many of God's rules did they ignore?

Q7. Should we be surprised or shocked at what happened to Uzzah?

Can you think of any similar incidents elsewhere in scripture?

Read Acts 5:1-5.

We have noted previously (page 10) how David reacted angrily to the LORD'S own holy anger. In 13:12, the Chronicler changes the focus to David being *afraid* rather than *angry*, to reinforce the lesson he wants us to learn.

Q8. How should we react to this incident?

Q9. What would you say to some-one who says,
"Oh, that was the God of the Old Testament!"?

> **Discuss:**
>
> Acts 5?
>
> 'The presumptuous sin of Uzzah was that that he assumed his hands were less polluted that the dirt (soil[24])' – R.C. Sproul

The ark is eventually brought to Jerusalem in 1 Chronicles 15. The account is greatly expanded over the one in 2 Samuel, with lots of named Levitical rôles, presumably for the benefit of the returned exiles as they re-instituted divine service at the re-built temple[25].

Q10. What signs are there that David has learned an important lesson about how to be a reverent king?

14:10

---

24   'Soil' in UK English.
25   Presumably without an actual ark of the covenant. It is assumed to have been destroyed with the temple in 586 BC.

15:2

Read 15:11-15.

Q11. Is David right to apportion a share of the blame for Uzzah's death to the *Levites* (Deuteronomy 17:18; Revelation 3:7)?

Application

King David's reign gets under way with a magnificent display of unity under his spiritually prioritised leadership. Eventually, there is great blessing, first (accidentally?) to the *household of Obed-Edom* (13:14), then to David through *Hiram king of Tyre* (14:1-2), followed by the defeat of some old enemies, the *Philistines* in 14:8-17.

1 Chronicles 14:2 And David knew that the LORD had established him as king over Israel, and that his kingdom was highly exalted for the sake of his people Israel.

In fact, King David became so great that:

14:17 ... the fame of David went out into all lands, and the LORD brought the fear of him upon all nations.

But, first some important leadership lessons had to be learned.

1. God is holy. They and the returned exiles later must remember this.

2. They must obey God's word, even if it was written down a long time ago.

3. The Levites should have been making sure that God's people, including the king, obeyed God's instructions.

King Jesus has left us very clear injunctions about obeying scripture, for example:

John 14:23 Jesus answered him, "If anyone loves me, he will keep my word, and my Father will love him, and we will come to him and make our home with him."

If we want to enjoy God's presence, joy and blessing, as typified by David wanting the ark to reside in Jerusalem with him, we too must be careful to obey God's word as revealed to us in the Bible.

Furthermore, the rôle that the Levites had to teach God's word (Deuteronomy 33:8-10; 2 Chronicles 17:8-9) remains important:

1 Timothy 5:17 Let the elders who rule well be considered worthy of double honour, especially those who labour in preaching and teaching.

If Uzzah's death still shocks us then we have a problem with God's holiness.

Study 4 ■

1 Chronicles 16 – Thankful but divided worship

David's heart attitude was godly, something emphasised in Samuel, but the heart attitude of Saul's daughter Michal was anything but. As 1 Chronicles 15 ends, we read that she despised David in her heart (1 Chronicles 15:29). Chapter 16 reveals more of David's heart for the LORD.

Read 1 Chronicles 16:1-7.

Q1. What kind of activities reveal a godly heart attitude to *the LORD* in these verses?

16:1   16:2-3

16:4   16:5-6

16:7

Q2. How do the verses above compare with Philippians 4:4-6?

Q3. Which activities might God's modern people be in danger of omitting?

Discuss:

David's psalm in 1 Chronicles 16:8-36 is contained in Psalms 96, 105 and 106, and may not have been available when Samuel was written, but the Chronicler, writing much later, includes this material here, to teach the returned exiles to take time to thank God for all his blessings, not just to pray about all their difficulties.

Read 16:8-36.

Q4. Can you see the concept of doxological evangelism in 16:8-13?

How should our worship affect outsiders?

Q5. Why might 16:14-18 be especially poignant for the returned exiles in Jerusalem?

Q6. How might the returned exiles surrounded by enemies turn 16:19-22 into prayer?

Q7. In what ways does the doxological evangelism go much further in 16:23-33?

Are any of these elements missing from our own evangelism or meetings?

Q8. How does the psalmist tell believers to "argue with God" in 16:34-36?

How should this affect our own praying? Does it?

Read 16:37-43.

Q9. What is odd, particularly about 16:39-42?

You may wish to refer to the map on page 23 to see where Gibeon is.

Q10. How many high priests are there at this point?

16:39   18:16

Application

So the chapter ends with all the worship of God being glorious, highly organised, very thankful, God-honouring in every way, and even evangelistic.

But, there is something wrong: The worship of God, whose presence is represented by the ark in its tent in is happening in *Jerusalem*, but all the burnt offerings and all the atonement for sin are happening where the tabernacle is, at a high place, miles away, in *Gibeon*.

All these elements must come together one day in Christ who, on one hand, shows us what God is like and, on the other, died to atone for his people's sin. With such disunity of the outward worship of God, the picture in Chronicles of the very gospel itself, completely fulfilled in Christ, is temporarily disrupted. Such an arrangement cannot be allowed to continue. A temple, which unites all the elements of the gospel on a single location is urgently needed, however that is not going to be David's task, but Solomon's – and also ours, *care*fully, but *build* we must:

1 Corinthians 3:10 According to the grace of God given to me, like a skilled master builder I laid a foundation, and someone else is building upon it. Let each one take care how he builds upon it.

In what areas are your quiet times, family devotions, small group meetings or worship services, weak?

Comforting, Enjoying God, Benediction (Blessing), Doxology (Praise), Singing songs and hymns to each other, Thanksgiving, Supplication, Evangelism, Sharing food/eating together, Training, Thanksgiving supplication, Rebuking, Teaching, Singing psalms to God, Encouraging

When visitors come to church, what do they see? Are we plainly enjoying our God? Do we have plenty to thank him for? Or are we fiddling with our phones and distracted by life's worries?

Do we keep in mind all the other opportunities to build each other up through the many different interactions that are possible (and biblical)?

Study 5 ■

1 Chronicles 17 – The promised everlasting king

If the OT books from Exodus to Judges contain the Old Covenant or Mosaïc Covenant and what happened to the people under that covenant, so the books from Ruth to the end of the OT focus their attention on the Davidic Covenant – God's covenant with David and Solomon, and what happened in God's kingdom up to just before King Jesus came[26]. The Old Covenant was still in force, hence what happened when David and the Levites ignored the directions in Numbers about how to carry the ark of the covenant. But, most of the content of these later OT books must be read in the context of God's covenant with David and Solomon. And the covenantal content is at its most intense[27] in two passages:

- 2 Chronicles 7 – the dedication of Solomon's temple; and here,
- 1 Chronicles 17 (bearing in mind that similar material exists in Samuel and Kings, of course. See the table on page 17.)

Read 1 Chronicles 17:1-2.

Q1. Which *Nathan* is this, given the others mentioned in 1 Chronicles?

3:5   11:38

14:4   17:1,2

This is apparently minor, but important given how many Harrys, Rons and Hermiones[28] there are in the entirely fictional *Harry Potter*™ books, for example.

---

26   The table in Appendix A – The Hebrew Bible (Tanak) on page 59 shows the original arrangement of the scrolls of the OT.
27   For a detailed discussion of where covenantal material is concentrated, see my *Covenants for Evangelicals*, Covenant Books uk, 2nd ed., 2022: https://www.amazon.co.uk/dp/B0B14HKXHM
28   Indeed there is a theory that JKR only wrote these novels to teach people how to pronounce the name 'Hermione'.

Q2. What does the fact that there are many duplicate place names and names of people in the biblical accounts tell us?

Q3. What big truth does Nathan state, whilst making what big mistake in 17:2?

Truth: Mistake:

Read 17:3-15.

That same night, *Nathan* functions as a *prophet* should (17:15), and reports to *David* in his *house of cedar* a message from *the* LORD (17:4-6).

Q4. What reason does *God* give for it really not being a problem that he wandered around with his *shepherd*-leaders with no temple in which to live (17:4,6)?

Also, notice the '24/7' way in which the book of Exodus ends:

Exodus 40:38 For the cloud of the LORD *was on the tabernacle by day, and fire was in it by night, in the sight of all the house of Israel throughout all their journeys.*

Model of the tabernacle,
Timna Park, Israel (By user Ruk7, Wikipedia)

Q5. How does the LORD continue the *shepherd*ing and agricultural themes in 17:7-9?

Why?

Q6. What does the word *'house'* mean in all these verses?
[building, family, dynasty, temple, household, ...]

10:6   13:14

14:1   17:1

The kings of the perfect kingdom 33

17:4   17:10

Q7. Who are verses 17:11-13 generally talking about?

Q8. Who is 17:14 specifically talking about, and what *kingdom* is this?

Read 17:16-27; David's prayer:
Q9. Given that praying is usually about asking, what does David ask?

Q10. What else does he do in 17:16-27?

17:16   17:17-19

17:20   17:21-22

17:23 Asks 'do what you promised'.   17:24

Q11. How should we respond when we find God's promises in the Bible?

17:25   17:25

17:27

Application

As with Nathan's casual blessing on David's building project, we should be wary of anyone claiming to have a 'word from the Lord':

Deuteronomy 18:21 ... 'How may we know the word that the LORD *has not spoken?'—* [22] *when a prophet speaks in the name of the* LORD, *if the word does not come to pass or come true, that is a word that the* LORD *has not spoken; the prophet has spoken it presumptuously. You need not be afraid of him.*

However, Nathan was also a genuine prophet of the Lord and brought David a lovely response to his desire to honour his God, 1 Chronicles 17:4-14, which forms the heart of what is often referred to as the Davidic Covenant.

1,000 years later, David's greatest son came, as promised (17:14), and made a special covenant with us:

Luke 22:20 ... "This cup that is poured out for you is the new covenant in my blood. [Jesus]

David made a magnificent response to God's covenant with him, but many Christians are unsure how to respond to receiving the bread and wine during the Lord's supper. This 'bookmark' may prove a helpful reminder:

	SAMPLE TWO PART PRAYER FOR USE DURING COMMUNION:
The Bread:	*"Lord Jesus, thank you for going to the cross for us, your people. I personally depend on your death for me, a sinner."*
The Cup:	*"Thank you for your promise of complete forgiveness. Assure me now of sins forgiven, and empower me to live my life for you."*

On the day of Pentecost, the apostle Peter goes further into the new covenant, specifically naming God the *Holy Spirit*, when he announces:

Acts 2:38 And Peter said to them, "Repent and be baptised every one of you in the name of Jesus Christ for the forgiveness of your sins, and you will receive the gift of the Holy Spirit. [39] For the promise[29] is for you and for your children and for all who are far off, everyone whom the Lord our God calls to himself."

Q12. How should we respond in prayer to such promises (as David did)?

Discuss:

Q13. How can scripture help us to pray in those areas of life or kingdom where we do not have specific promises?

Discuss:

---

29   Notice here the covenant language being used: *'repent'; 'the name of'; 'promise'; 'you and your children'; 'for ever'.*

Study 6 ■

1 Chronicles 18-20 – The victory of the messianic king

To show how David's kingdom grew dramatically in these chapters, there is a map on page 35 showing many of the places named.

This next period of David's reign is one that must have brought sighs, groans and tears to the returned exiles in Jerusalem 500 years later. The events included in Samuel are incredibly discouraging things: the backward-looking story of Mephibosheth (Saul's grandson); David's adultery; the rape of Tamar by Amnon; the death of Amnon; Absalom's attempted coup and death. Presumably the Chronicler realises that these well-known events will do nothing to strengthen and encourage his readers so, instead, he focuses on David's victories in battle. In the same way that David trusted God, obeyed him and received answers to prayer and promises fulfilled, so the occupants of the derelict Jerusalem trying to rebuild the temple needed to be reminded of what God can do for his people, especially as they looked forward to the coming of the promised messianic king one day – rather like us, really.

Q1. Whilst being careful to make sure that we do read the whole Bible and do not miss out the parts that we find uncomfortable, how can we read the Bible in the way that is most helpful to us at any stage of our lives and experience so that we find help in time of need, encouragement, rebuke or whatever is most apt?

Discuss:

Read 1 Chronicles 18:1-6,12-13. Find these battles on the map.

Q2. Which promises are starting to be fulfilled?

17:8

17:9

17:10

Numbers 24:18

Read chapter 19 (noting places on the map).

Q3. When *Hanun son of Nahash* treated *David* so rudely and his *messengers* so shamefully, how might *David* have felt about whether *God* was keeping his promises?

The kings of the perfect kingdom

Q4. How did things only seem to get worse in verses 6 and 7?

Whilst *Joab*, David's nephew and a man not known for his fear of God, issues a rare spiritual command (19:13), he notices that things have got even worse in that his troops are now surrounded.

Q5. After a perhaps surprisingly successful *battle*, how do things get worse yet again in 19:16?

By the end of chapter 19, David is entirely victorious, but this chapter of his reign had been far from straightforward. At this point, we are tempted to look back into 2 Samuel 10 to see if God was chastising David a bit for his sin! No such luck. Sometimes, like David, we just have to keep trusting and obeying God, even when he seems to be making life difficult for us, knowing that one day, somehow, he will grant us victory. Not all discipline or hardship or trials are chastisements for our sin.

Hebrews 12:7 Endure hardship as discipline; God is treating you as his children. For what children are not disciplined by their father? NIV

Q6. How might David have found Hebrews 12:7[30] helpful during the stresses and strains of 1 Chronicles 19?

Read 20:1-3.

Q7. What emphasis (picked up from 18:7;11) is continued in this section?

Q8. Was this the end of the *Ammonites*? Not yet, but see Ezekiel 25:10.

Read 20:4-8. Notice how the Chronicler recalls one of *David's* early victories.

Q9. What is the emphasis in this section? **Clue**: The *Rephaites* (NIV) were *giants*. In 20:4,6,8, The ESV actually renders '*Repha(im)*' as '*giant(s)*'.

Q10. Can you think of examples of 'giant' enemies that Christians face today?

Discuss:

---
30   I know!

Q11. What happened to the Philistines in the end? See Jeremiah 47:1-4.

Application

For David, the Ammonites, Rephaites (giants) and Philistines continued to be enemies, although he largely subdued them all in these three chapters, so before 970 BC.

The returned exiles in Jerusalem however, around perhaps 450 BC, could perhaps see for themselves the final defeat of these enemies. It is not absolutely certain by which years they had disappeared at the hands of Egypt and Babylon. We, however, will struggle to find any evidence of Philistines, Ammonites and Rephaites today, except in museums.

Philistine clay death mask from 11th century BC or earlier, British Museum, Photo © David W. Legg 2004

Will King Jesus achieve even greater victory over his enemies than David did? His style may often be different, but the result is the same:

Matthew 12:20 a bruised reed he will not break, and a smouldering wick he will not quench, until he brings justice to victory.

Nevertheless, like David's, Jesus' *victory* was a bloody one on the cross. But he conquered *death*:

1 Corinthians 15:55 "O death, where is your victory? O death, where is your sting?"

and then gives the *victory* to his people:

1 Corinthians 15:57 But thanks be to God, who gives us the victory through our Lord Jesus Christ.

The struggling returned exiles in Jerusalem awaited the same messianic king as we do. The difference is, we await his second coming and can see clearly in the NT how his *victory* was achieved. They had to keep serving in a small way in the temple, in Jerusalem, and their faithfulness was eventually rewarded when the Messiah came: Simeon in the second temple, holding the messianic baby:

Luke 2:30 ... my eyes have seen your salvation ... (Nunc dimittis)

Study 7 ■

1 Chronicles 21:1–22:1 – A mystery and the heart of the gospel

The Chronicler must have considered this material very important to repeat almost all the same material from Samuel and expand on it, but the alert reader will immediately notice a problem that should not be skipped over.

1 Chronicles 21:1 Then Satan stood against Israel and incited David to number [i.e. count, take a census of] *Israel.*
2 Samuel 24:1 Again the anger of the LORD was kindled against Israel, and he incited David against them, saying, "Go, number [i.e. count] Israel and Judah."

The chapter begins in a fascinating way, because in the previous account in Samuel it is the LORD how incites *David* to sin, but here it is *Satan* who did it.

Q1. How can we tease out a possible scenario that explains both verses?

Do Genesis 50:20 and Romans 8:28 help at all? See also James 1:13-15. A possible scenario is outlined in the Application section on page 42.

Read 1 Chronicles 21:1-7, then Exodus 30:11-16.

Q2. How was *David's* sinful command similar to what went wrong in 1 Chronicles 13 resulting in *Uzzah's* death? See page 24. on 1 Chronicles 13:7-10. Also notice the strong terms used in Exodus 30:12,16 *ransom*, *atonement*.

Q3. What ceremony has God given us to make sure we do not forget about the need for our *sins* to be atoned for (Matthew 26:28)?

Read 1 Chronicles 21:8-14.

It is worth reflecting once again on how Chronicles is certainly not a whitewashed account of King David! See 21:30 too.

Q4. David's majestic theological statement in 21:13 should give us pause for thought. How should this great truth affect us nowadays?

Discuss:

Read 1 Chronicles 21:15-16.

Q5. Despite God's *very great mercy* (21:13), a lot of people die (21:14). Is God acting unjustly?

Romans 3:23

Romans 6:23

Q6. How is David's reliance on God's *very great mercy* rewarded?

The Dead Sea Scrolls from 300 BC to 100 AD and the Septuagint[2] from ~250 BC make it probable that the Hebrew of 21:17 was originally[31]:

And David said to God, "Was it not I who gave command to number the people? It is I [the shepherd] who have sinned and done great evil. But these sheep, what have they done? Please let your hand, O LORD my God, be against me and against my father's house. But do not let the plague be on your people."

The textual variant add the words *'the shepherd'* which make *David's* exclamation even more poignant and deeply theological. Looking at verse 17, how does *David* try to deflect God's anger and take the sin on himself?

---
31 Something similar is probably true of verse 16, which is normally included without a footnote in English translations. See the concise note on 21:116 in the *NIV Study Bible*, 1984 version, Zondervan, 1987.

v17 These [are but] *sheep. What have they done?*

v17 Let your hand be against me …

v17 … and on my father's house (i.e. David's family line)

Q7. How does David compare with Jesus in John 18:7-8?

Q8. Where did all the sin that was stored up for 1,000 years by David's prayer go ultimately?

"Please let your hand, O LORD my God, be against me and against my father's house (i.e. David's family line)." v17

Q9. In showing that *Jesus* is descended from *King David*, how does Matthew 1 explain what is going on in 1 Chronicles 21:17, especially Matthew 1:21?

Matthew 1:21

Read 21:18-30.
Araunah (same name as *Ornan*) mistakenly tries to help with making atonement for the sin of God's people in 21:23.

Q10. Why would it have been wrong for David to accept any such help?

Think about Jesus, and what he had to do alone on the cross.

Psalm 49:7 Truly no man can ransom another, or give to God the price of his life, [8] for the ransom of their life is costly and can never suffice, [9] that he should live on for ever and never see the pit.

Psalm 49:7-9 makes it clear that that would be impossible for a ordinary human king like David. But Jesus is no ordinary king:

2 Corinthians 5:21 For our sake [God] *made him to be sin who knew no sin, so that in him we might become the righteousness of God.*

Read 22:1.
And later, in 2 Chronicles 3:1, King Solomon builds the temple on Mount

Moriah, where sacrifices are offered for 1,000 years for sin, in exactly the same place that King David had used to sacrifice in 1 Chronicles 21:26.

Application

In terms of how best to reconcile 2 Samuel 24:1 and 1 Chronicles 21:1, we should first recognise that we are not given enough information to be absolutely sure, so some guesswork is required that must keep within the bounds of what scripture allows.

2 Samuel 24:1 Again the anger of the LORD *was kindled against Israel, ...*

Presumably, Israel had started worshipping idols (or another of their besetting sins), so the LORD decides to chastise them. In order to do that he decides to use, first, Satan, then perhaps other members of David's staff, and lastly David himself. So, perhaps God (somehow, we are not told exactly how he *incited* David) gets one of David's entourage to mention that, say, the Arameans (Syrians) have a bigger army than Israel. This arouses David's (sinful) envy, so, ...

1 Chronicles 21:2 David said to Joab and the commanders of the army, "Go, number Israel, ...

When we take the long view, we see God working all these machinations together for his own glory and for the good of his people (Romans 8:28): They receive a majestic temple as a centre for worship (1 Chronicles 28ff).

We must also not accuse God of actually *tempting* David (James 1:13-15). The word *'incited'* (2 Samuel 24:1) does not mean 'temped directly'. He is quite capable of working human (and Satanic) sin into his plans in such a way that the responsibility remains with the sinner, but the plan still produces good (Genesis 50:20), as with *Joseph* and his brothers in Egypt. So, we do not know all the detail, but that is one possible scenario.

All this rather begs the question, 'What should we do when someone claims to have found a contradiction in the Bible and proceeds to explain how it is therefore unreliable as a guide for faith and life?'[32]

Discuss:

---

32 Chapter 1 'Of the Holy Scripture' in *The Westminster Confession of Faith*, 1646/7 is well worth a read to clarify our doctrine of scripture. Its authors, the seventeenth century *Westminster Assembly of Divines* consisted of ministers, theologians, and others of the English and Scottish churches. The English parliament originally appointed this council from 1643–1653 to reform the liturgy, discipline, and government of the Church of England.

Study 8 ■

1 Chronicles 22:1-19 – Solomon king of peace

Previously, chapter 16 ended with a tension: As David and all the people went to their homes, the house of the LORD was divided between Gibeon where the tabernacle was and Jerusalem where the ark of the covenant lived temporarily in a tent provided by David. The LORD was homeless!

Matthew 8:20 And Jesus said ..., "Foxes have holes, and birds of the air have nests, but the Son of Man has nowhere to lay his head."

Read 1 Chronicles 22:1 again.

Q1. How does 22:1 resolve the tension left over from the end of chapter 16 described above?

22:1

22:19

Read 22:2-5.

Q2. What is interesting about who did much of the work and provided much of the material needed to start building God's temple in Jerusalem (see also Genesis 27:29)?

22:2   22:4b

Q3. Who are meant to see Solomon's temple?

22:5

Read 22:6-10 noting that Solomon's name means 'peace', like 'shalom'.

Q4. Was it just because David was too busy (1 Kings 5:3) that he was disallowed from building the temple?

22:8

Q5. What reasons are given for Solomon to be the temple's builder?

22:9

Q6. Although a repeat from chapter 17:12-14, why is 22:10 so important theologically?

Mark 1:11   Luke 1:32-33

Hebrews 1:5

Q7. How does it make sense that Solomon's throne would last for ever (22:10)? See also Hebrews 1:8.

Read 22:11-13.

Q8. What great covenant promise and condition are in these verses?

22:12

22:13

Read 22:14-19.

Q9. Apart from Solomon himself, how many different parties were involved with building the first temple?

22:14   22:15

22:17   22:18

The kings of the perfect kingdom 45

Q10. Who is involved with *building* the body of Christ, the *church*?

John 2:19-21 (*raise* ESV, *build* NIV)　　Matthew 16:18

Acts 4:11　　Ephesians 4:11-12

1 Peter 2:5　　Romans 15:2

Application

The temple to be built was not only a 'type' of Jesus' body (John 2:19-21), but even had Jesus as its cornerstone (Acts 4:11). Furthermore, the unity of Christ with his people means that the temple is also a type (1 Peter 2:5) of the church (Ephesians 4:12). We are all involved in building the church (Romans 15).

Not only is Jesus often called the Son of David, but we discover here that Solomon too is a 'type' of Christ. By his reign, his wisdom (2 Chronicles 1; 9) and, especially, his temple he was the supreme man of peace. On his own, David was an inadequate type of Christ. His contribution to typology needed to be supplemented by that of Solomon and many others.

Q11. Can you think of some of the others?

We have already noted Simeon's 'nunc dimittis' in Luke 2:28-32, but we should note some more of its features when we remember Solomon's temple being built (partly) by the *nations*, so be seen by *all nations*, and when we remember <u>where</u> it was that Simeon first met Jesus:

*Luke 2:27 Moved by the Spirit, he went into **the temple** courts ... ²⁸ Simeon took him in his arms and praised God, saying:*
²⁹ "Sovereign Lord, as you have promised,
　[you may] now dismiss[i.e. nunc dimittis in Latin] *your servant in **peace**.*
³⁰ For my eyes have seen your salvation,
*³¹　which you have prepared in the sight of all **nations**:*
*³² a light for revelation to the **Gentiles**,*
　*and the glory of your people **Israel**."*

Those of us who are Gentiles, together with any of Jewish descent, should worshipfully thank *God* for how his amazing plan, pictured in Chronicles, all came together to grant us peace with God through King Jesus:

Acts 10:36;	1 Peter 1:2;	1 Timothy 1:2;
Romans 1:7; 5:1; 16:20;	1 Thessalonians 1:1; 5:23;	2 Timothy 1:2;
1 Corinthians 1:3;	2 Thessalonians 1:2;	Titus 1:4;
2 Corinthians 1:2;	Philippians 1:2; 4:7;	2 Peter 1:2;
Galatians 1:3;	Philemon 3;	2 John 1:3.
Ephesians 1:2;	Hebrews 13:20-21;	

If the importance of *peace* can be measured by this length of this list of blessing texts (benedictions), we should pay much greater attention to every benediction at the end of every service to make sure that we receive by faith the promised *peace* that was bought by King Jesus at such a high price, and modelled by King Solomon's magnificent temple.

Study 9 ■

1 Chronicles 23-27 – Levites and the priesthood of all believers

Previously, the Levites had been scattered around Israel to teach the Israelites[33]. Many of them had also been kept in reserve to carry the (movable) tabernacle and all its sacred contents[34]. So, Solomon's (immovable) temple now made many Levites redundant (23:26)! Whilst all the detail in these chapters is not so relevant to modern Christians, it was all important to the returned exiles who were trying to re-establish the right God-given rôles surrounding temple worship and the security of Jerusalem.

Read 1 Chronicles 23:1-6.

Q1. What numbers give an indication of the sheer scale of the temple operation?

Cast an eye over chapter 23 and identify the three divisions of Levites.

_____   _____   _____

Read 23:24-27.

Previously, under what we now call the Old Covenant (2 Corinthians 3:14), the covenant representative was Moses who set up all the arrangements for worship at the tabernacle in Exodus, Leviticus and Numbers. With the failure, and decline in importance, of the Old Covenant, and with worship moving from the tabernacle[35] to the temple, the new, Davidic, covenant gave the messianic kings[36] the authority[37] to change how the people worshipped God. The Levites were always central to how worship happened in Israel.

33　A function that seems to have been reinstated by 2 Chronicles 35:3.
34　As per Numbers 4.
35　See the photograph on page 32.
36　Not only David and Solomon, but also, notably, Hezekiah.
37　Indeed, 1 Chronicles 28:12 gives a fascinating insight into the divine origin even of David's plans for Solomon's temple. This parallels the giving of the plans for the tabernacle to Moses in Exodus 25-30.

Q2. What significant adjustment was needed to provide enough Levites for Solomon's magnificent and glorious temple?

23:27

Read 24:6; 19.

Most church members are familiar with the idea of rôtas for serving.

Q3. Who took responsibility for organising this particular rôta in verses 7-18 (24:6; 31)?

Read 25:1; 26:12-20; 27-29; 32.

Q4. What other jobs did *David* allocate to all these many other *Levites*?

David also commanded the army, of course, and there is a list of other rôles in 27:25ff.

Read 27:23-24.

The Chronicler reveals one of his many source documents in 27:24:

Others include:

the Pentateuch,	*Jeremiah,*	'the annotations on the book of the kings',
Judges,	*Lamentations,*	
Ruth,	*Zechariah,*	'Nathan the prophet',
Psalms,	'the book of the kings of Israel',	'Ahijah the Shilonite',
Isaiah,		'Iddo the seer', and
Samuel,	'the book of the kings of Judah and Israel',	'Shemaiah the prophet'.
Kings,		

Q5. What kind of writer was the Chronicler, and what kind of book is Chronicles? From where did his authority come?

Q6. What kind of things does our covenant representative, King Jesus, have authority to change?

Matthew 12:8   Matthew 9:38

Matthew 9:6   Matthew 28:18-20

The kings of the perfect kingdom 49

Mark 1:27	Luke 9:1
John 5:27	John 10:18
John 17:2	Revelation 2:26-27

Application

Levites are not mentioned much in the NT.

Q7. What do we learn from this *Levite* (parable of the good Samaritan)?

Luke 10:32 So likewise a Levite, when he came to the place and saw him, passed by on the other side.

Q8. What do we learn from this *Levite* (John the baptist)?

John 1:19 And this is the testimony of John [himself a Levite], when the Jews sent priests and Levites from Jerusalem to ask him, "Who are you?"

Q9. What do we learn from this *Levite*?

Acts 4:36 ... Joseph, who was also called by the apostles Barnabas (which means son of encouragement), a Levite, a native of Cyprus, [37] sold a field that belonged to him and brought the money and laid it at the apostles' feet.

Given the relative absence in scripture of Levites since Jesus, it is obvious that the rôle is to be performed by Christians. It would also seem that it is specifically[38] the rôle known as the 'priesthood of all believers' that is to be filled.

Read 1 Peter 2:1-12, and pick out what is required of New Covenant priests.

2:1

2:2

---
38 Priests also being Levites, but with other specific tasks. See Leviticus.

2:5

2:6

2:8 (negative)

2:9

2:11

2:12

Homework: Look up all the other NT verses about *priests* using a Bible concordance.

Study 10 ■

1 Chronicles 28-29 – David's and Solomon's hearts

As in any relay race there is a hand-over of a baton. But this time, the b being run is the messianic kingship of God's people, and the equivalent of a baton is a set of plans for the building of God's temple.

The Chronicler shows how King David 'finished well'. In particular, he exposes David's heart attitudes through various speeches. The big questions are,

'Will Solomon drop the baton?'

and

'Does Solomon have the same godly heart as his father?'

David's first speech is to all his staff and army with, presumably, Solomon sitting there too.

Read 1 Chronicles 28:1-8.

Q1. What do we learn about David's heart and the kind of heart attitudes he demands of his people?

28:2   28:3

28:8

Q2. Why does the Chronicler particularly include mention of the tribe of *Judah* and the royal line of succession through *Solomon* for the returned exiles to read?

28:4   9:1,3

Genesis 49:10   28:5-7

Q3. Looking at 28:8, why did the returned exiles not have the land as their inheritance for ever?

Luke 13:34-35

Q4. How is 28:8 expanded into a much greater promise, in Christ?

Romans 4:13   Matthew 5:5

David then specifically address Solomon.

Read 28:9-13.

Q5. Again, how does David highlight the importance of Solomon's heart attitudes?

28:9   28:9

28:10   28:20

David then turns his attention to the whole assembly, because Solomon is young and inexperienced.

Read 29:1-9.

Q6. Now whose heart attitudes are revealed?

29:2   29:3

29:6   29:9

Notice how heart attitudes also affect the wallet.

Read 29:10-20.

Q7. What are the main features of David's doxology in verses 10-13 and the prayer that follows?

PRAISE	THANKSGIVING	PRIDE	REPENTANCE
HISTORY	DOUBT	HONESTY	DEVOTION
WORSHIP	FAITH	CONCERN	ABANDON
COMMANDS	HUMILITY	JOY	OBEDIENCE

Q8. Which of the above are also godly heart attitudes?

Q9. What is the big heart-question that David has for Solomon and his people?

29:17

29:18

29:19

Notice how David's concern was not limited to the external things like whether the temple would actually get built. The big issue from the very beginning of his reign is still the big issue when he hands the baton on:

Acts 13:22 [Paul speaking in Pisidian Antioch:] *And when he had removed [Saul], he raised up David to be their king, of whom he testified and said, 'I have found in David the son of Jesse a man after my heart, who will do all my will.'*

Application

The big question is whether *Solomon* will prove to be like *David* or like *Saul*. The big question is still the heart-question.

And the big question for us too is a heart-question. The question is not what have you done, but why did you do it?

Read 1 Corinthians 13:1-7.

Q10. What things does Paul label as worthless?

Q11. How, practically, does love express itself (13:4-7)?

Look up and meditate on these texts:

Matthew 5:8	Matthew 6:21
Matthew 13:15	Matthew 15:18
Matthew 22:37	Galatians 4:6

The Kingdom of Solomon

Study 11 ∎

2 Chronicles 1-2 – Solomon seeks God's kingdom (at) first

King Solomon inherited an *exceedingly great kingdom* (2 Chronicles 1:1) from his father David in 970 BC. But, what was needed to establish such a kingdom in godliness? A combination of great wisdom, great blessing and a glorious temple – the sign and seal of the Davidic Covenant that God made with the messianic kings of Israel and Judah.

Read 2 Chronicles 2:1-17.

Q1. Why did *Solomon* seek God's blessing in 1:5 on Mount *Gibeon*? (The map may help.)

Q2. Why did *Solomon* offer *burnt offerings* (1:6; see Leviticus 1:4)?

And why *1,000* (1:2-3)?

Q3. Does John 15:7 throw any light on 1:7?

Q4. What can we learn for ourselves from *Solomon's* prayer in 1:8-10?

1:8

1:9

1:10

Matthew 6:33 (below)

Matthew 6:33 But seek first the kingdom of God and his righteousness, and all these things will be added to you.

Q5. What *things* were *added* in Solomon's case?

1:11   1:11

1:11   1:11

1:11

See the above map for the locations of the sources of some of Solomon's unexpected answers to his kingdom-centred prayer.

As we proceed into 2 Chronicles, we should also note that it has even more to say about the importance of our hearts than 1 Chronicles, with more than twice as many references to the heart[39].

Read 2:1-6.

Q6. What clues are there to the sheer scale of the temple building operation?

Q7. Why did the temple (*house*) need to be so *great*?

2:5

Q8. And yet, of what is *Solomon's* temple to be just a tiny model ('type')?

2:6

And so, Solomon handles greatness (1:1) with humility (2:6). How is it possible for someone to be both great and humble? It seems a straightforward contradiction to us.

Of whom is Solomon, like David, a picture, a 'type' – someone much greater who humbled himself far more?

Isaiah 53:3

---
39   Something like 34 to 13, but there is more than one Hebrew word for heart.

2 Corinthians 8:9

Philippians 2:8

2 Chronicles 2:11 Then Hiram the king of Tyre answered in a letter that he sent to Solomon, "Because the LORD loves his people, he has made you king over them."

Application

King Solomon gets off to a great start by *seeking first God* and *his kingdom*. Wisdom is not something only needed by kings:

James 1:5 If any of you lacks wisdom, let him ask God, who gives generously to all without reproach, and it will be given him.

Q9. In what situations do we need wisdom from God?

Discuss:

A friend recently asked me to pray this prayer with him daily for a few months:

Colossians 1:9 And so, from the day we heard, we have not ceased to pray for you, asking that you may be filled with the knowledge of his will in all spiritual wisdom and understanding, ⁱ⁰ so as to walk in a manner worthy of the Lord, fully pleasing to him, bearing fruit in every good work and increasing in the knowledge of God.

Q10. How does Paul's prayer add to a simple a request for divine *wisdom*?

Q11. What might we expect from our *God* when we ask in this way?

Ephesians 3:20 Now to him who is able to do far more abundantly than all that we ask or think, according to the power at work within us, ^{21} to him be glory in the church and in Christ Jesus throughout all generations, for ever and ever. Amen.

How often is the problem that we simply did not ask (James 4:2)?

Study 12 ■

2 Chronicles 3-6 – The perfect house of God

It is the spring of 966 BC, and King Solomon has finally imported enough resources in terms of materials and workers to begin building a house for the LORD.

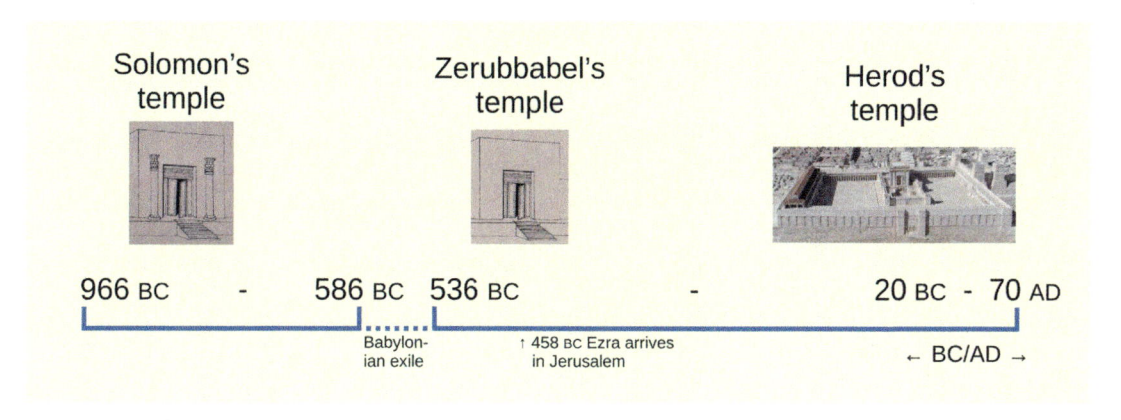

Solomon's temple	Zerubbabel's temple	Herod's temple
966 BC – 586 BC	536 BC –	20 BC - 70 AD
	Babylonian exile	↑ 458 BC Ezra arrives in Jerusalem	← BC/AD →

Read 2 Chronicles 3:1-2.

Q1. What is the significance of the temple's location?

Genesis 22:2

1 Chronicles 21:25-22:1

Q2. Does the latter reference give any clues as to the main purpose of the temple? Bear in mind that this location was perhaps a few hundred yards away from where Jesus would be crucified:

Hebrews 13:12 So Jesus also suffered outside the gate in order to sanctify the people through his own blood.

The ark of the covenant was covered in gold and represented God's presence among his people.

Read 3:3-5:1, counting the number of references to gold: _____

Q3. What general impression did you receive of God's temple (*house*)?

Q4. What impression did you receive of the God whose home it was to be?

Q5. What significant features of the temple did you notice?

3:8	3:10
3:14	3:17
4:1	4:18
4:19	

Q6. By 5:1, what was missing?

Read 5:2-10.

Q7. Which *covenant* is being referred to in 5:2, 5:7 and 5:10?

Read 5:13-6:2.

Q8. How would the references to 'for ever' (5:13; 6:2) be helpful to the returned exiles in Jerusalem as they rebuilt the temple or re-established worship there?

Almost all the references to God's promises in 2 Chronicles are in chapter 6.

Q9. What is the significance of each promise for them and for us?

6:4

6:10

6:16

6:20

Remember to think of Jesus being the complete fulfilment of the temple.

Q10. Whose prayers towards or in the temple will be answered, and in what circumstances?

6:21	6:24
6:26	6:28-29
6:32-33	6:34-35

6:38-39

Application

In 586 BC and then again in 70 AD the temple was destroyed, and its site is currently under another, Muslim, building. How can Christians pray towards the temple in Jerusalem nowadays? Do we need to write prayers on tiny rolls of paper and push them into the 'wailing wall'[40] as some Jews do?

Happily:

1 Corinthians 3:16 Do you not know that you are God's temple and that God's Spirit dwells in you?

---

[40] The wailing wall is the only part of the temple that remains today, and is actually only really amongst the foundations holding the temple on the temple mount?

Notice how a better, and more exclusive altar, is now available to the readers of Hebrews. Also, notice how he reveals the identity of that altar in 13:12 and urges us to approach God though Jesus in 13:13:

Hebrews 13:10 We have an altar from which those who serve the tent have no right to eat. ... ¹² So Jesus also suffered outside the gate in order to sanctify the people through his own blood. ¹³ Therefore let us go to him outside the camp and bear the reproach he endured.

Furthermore, God's spiritual temple, Jesus' church, is still being built:

Ephesians 2:21 in whom [Jesus] *the whole structure, being joined together, grows into a holy temple in the Lord.*

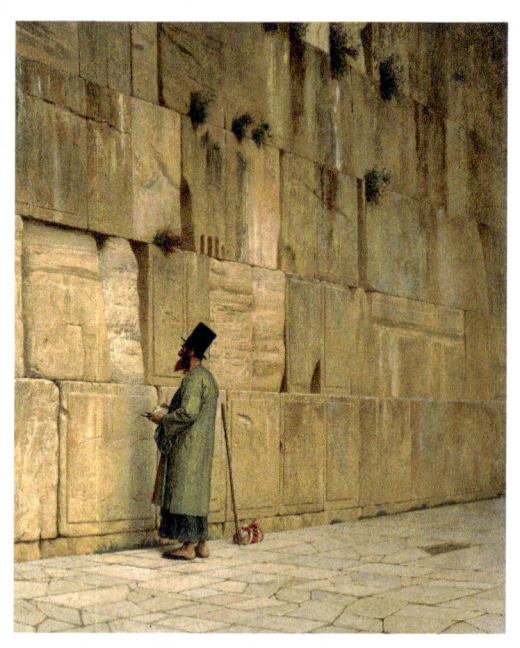

'The Wailing Wall' – Painting by J.L. Gerome (1824 – 1904)
Wikimedia Commons, Public domain

And one day:

Revelation 21:22 And I saw no temple in the city, for its temple is the Lord God the Almighty and the Lamb.

This is possible because Jesus is the perfect temple.

Study 13 ■

2 Chronicles 7-9 – Solomon, the perfect king?

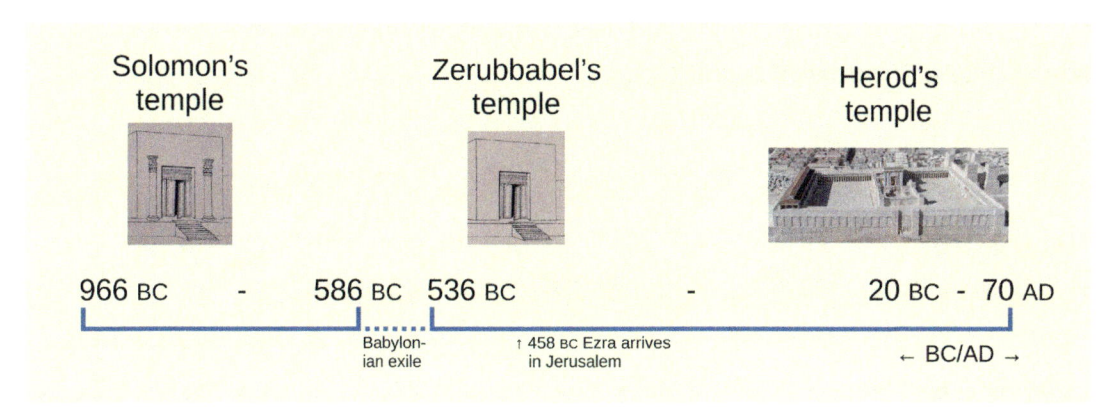

The single greatest sign and seal of Solomon's kingship and of God keeping his promises to David was the 'first' temple, unifying the worship of the one true God which had previously been split between the ark in Jerusalem and the tabernacle in Gibeon. So, in 959 BC, Solomon's temple superseded the tabernacle and incorporated the ark of the covenant (2 Chronicles 5:2-14).

Much later, in 516 BC, when the 'second' temple was completed, it was a much less grand temple than Solomon's – so much so that the people who saw even the foundations being laid actually wept (Ezra 3:12). Although everyone was ceremonially clean, the passover was kept and the LORD filled them all with joy (Ezra 6:19-22), everything was on a much smaller scale and less dramatic: There were many fewer burnt offerings, and God's presence was much less obvious. How these returned exiles needed to be reminded of the historical reality of the glory days that were their heritage!

Read 2 Chronicles 5:14; 7:1-12.

Q1. Back in 959 BC, when the first *temple* was dedicated, how were things much more glorious?

5:14   7:1

7:1-2	7:3
7:5 (compared with Ezra 6:17)	7:7

Q2. If some of the returned *exiles* in 516 BC (Ezra 6:15[41]) were thinking to themselves, 'The LORD really let us down when Solomon's temple was destroyed in 586 BC[37], maybe we will have more luck with this second temple', what might the LORD reply?

Read 7:17-22 (spoken in 959 BC).

Daniel 9:2

Read 8:1-6.

Q3. What impression are we given here of *Solomon's* reign?

Read 9:1-8.

Q4. What does the *Queen of Sheba*[42] discover?

9:1	9:2-3
9:5	9:6
9:7	9:8 (Notice who got the glory)

Read 9:13;22-31.

Q5. What further impressions do we get of *Solomon's* reign?

9:1	9:22

9:26 (see map)

---
41 This was pretty well exactly 70 years after its destruction. See Daniel 9:2.
42 Possibly modern Yemen.

Read Luke 11:29-32.

Q6. What does this passage teach us about the *Queen's* possible spiritual progress though meeting *King Solomon*?

Luke 11:31

Q7. What does *Jesus'* use of *Jonah* and the *Queen* teach us about how we should expect to be able to learn from characters in the OT?

Luke 11:30

Luke 11:32

Luke 24:27

Q8. What important and practical lessons should we learn from the *Queen* ourselves?

2 Chronicles 9:1   2 Chronicles 9:3-4

2 Chronicles 9:5   2 Chronicles 9:8

Psalm 34:8

Cast an eye over 1 Kings 11.
The prophet Jonah and the messianic kings, including David and Solomon are known as 'types' of Christ. As they were prophets and kings, so they teach us about Jesus, the ultimate prophet and king. Types are never perfect. Think, for example, of Jonah's disobedience (Jonah 1:3). Notice all Solomon's weaknesses and sin in 1 Kings 11. God and scripture never allow mere types of Christ to be perfect pictures of the real thing. The absolute glory is always reserved for Jesus himself.

Q9. How does the Chronicler missing out the material from 1 Kings 11 help us to see more clearly King Solomon as a type of King Jesus? See also the table on page 17.

Discuss:

Application

The returned exiles in Jerusalem were faced with an impoverished temple, limited wealth for sacrifices and offerings, and no glorious king (just a governor, see Haggai 1:1). There was not a whiff of divine fire or smoke when they dedicated the second temple. They needed to relive some of the glory of Solomon's reign and his majestic temple. This was no exercise in nostalgia; they needed the encouragement to remain faithful and serve God during the *'day of small things'* (Zechariah 4:10) until the longed-for Messiah King came that all Solomon's glory pointed forward to. Even the ark of the covenant seems to have gone missing. Its last historical mention is in 2 Chronicles 35:3. The people in Ezra's time must have found it very hard to believe that the LORD was actually with them!

Q10. How is our situation nowadays similar, but much better?

Discuss:

Matthew 12:6

Matthew 28:18-20

Philippians 3:20

1 Corinthians 10:11

John 14:16-18

1 Thessalonians 4:16-18

Homework: Read Psalm 72.

4 The division of the perfect kingdom

King/Queen of Judah	King of Israel/Samaria	Prophet	About	2 Chronicles	Kings
Rehoboam, Shishak?	Jeroboam I	Shemaiah, Iddo, Ahijah, others	Division of the kingdom	10:1–11:23	1 Kings ↓ 12:1–33
			Man of God from Judah warns Jeroboam I (Israel)		13:1–34
			Ahijah's prophecy against Jeroboam I (Israel)		14:1–18
			Death of Jeroboam I (Israel)		14:19–20
			Shishak (Egypt) attacks Jerusalem	12:1–12	14:25–28
		Iddo	Rehoboam (Judah)	12:13–16	14:21–24, 29–31
Abijah			War between Abijah (Judah) and Jeroboam I (Israel)	13:1–22	15:1–8
Asa		Oded	Early, godly, reign of Asa (Judah)	14:1–8	15:9–12
			Ethiopians defeated	14:9–15	
		Azariah	Azariah the prophet	15:1–7	
		Oded	Asa's reforms	15:8–19	15:13–15
		Jehu, Hanani	Asa's decline	16:1–10	15:16–22
			Asa's disease and death	16:11–14	15:23–24
	Nadab		Nadab		15:25–31
	Baasha		Baasha		15:32-16:7
	Elah	Jehu	Elah		16:8-14
	Zimri		Zimri		16:15-20
	Tibni		Tibni		16:21-22
	Omri		Omri		16:23-28
Jehoshaphat	Ahab		Ahab becomes king (Israel)		16:29–34
		Elijah/Obadiah+100	Elijah		17:1–19:18; 21:17–29
		Elijah, Micaiah, Jehu?	The call of Elisha		19:19–21
			Ahab attacks Samaria, defeats Ben-Hadad; Naboth's vineyard		20:1–21:29
			The godliness of Jehoshaphat (Judah); expansion of Judah	17:1–19	
		Micaiah, false prophets	Jehoshaphat's alliance with Ahab; death of Ahab	18:1–34	22:1–40
		Hanani, Jehu?	Jehoshaphat rebuked, his reforms, defeat of Moab and Ammon	19:1–20:30	
			Jehoshaphat's alliance with Ahaziah (Israel), and death	20:31–21:3	22:41–50
	Ahaziah	Elijah, others	Ahaziah (Israel)		22:51–53
			Death of Ahaziah; Elijah's prophecy		2 Kings ↓ 1:1–18
		Elijah, Elisha, others	Elijah translated; Elisha takes over		2:1–25

...

King/Queen of Judah	King of Israel/Samaria	Prophet	About	2 Chronicles	Kings
	J(eh)oram[44]	Elisha others	Moab rebels against J(eh)oram[44] (Israel)		3:1–27
			The widow's oil		4:1–7
			The Shunammite woman		4:8–37
			Miracles for the prophets		4:38–44
			Naaman healed		5:1–27
			The axe head recovered		6:1–7
			Chariots of fire		6:8–23
			Siege of Samaria		6:24–7:20
			Shunammite's land restored		8:1–6
			Hazael kills Ben-Hadad		8:7–15
Jehoram		Elijah (by letter)	Edom and Libnah rebel against Jehoram (Judah)	21:4–11	8:16–22
			Warning of Elijah	21:12–15	
			Invasion of Philistia and Arabia	21:16–17	
		Elisha others	Death of Jehoram	21:18–20	8:23–24
Ahaziah			Ahaziah (Judah)	22:1–9	8:25–29; 9:15–16, 27–28; 10:12–14
	Jehu		Jehu (Israel)	22:7–9	9:1–10:36
Athaliah			Athaliah (Judah)	22:10–23:15	11:1–16
			Jehoiada's reforms (Judah)	23:16–21	11:17–20
Joash			Joash (Judah) repairs the temple, good early reign	24:1–14	11:21–12:16
			Death of Jehoiada	24:15–16	
			Jehoiada's son killed, Joash's late ungodly reign	24:17–22	
			Syria invades Judah	24:23–24	12:17–18
			Death of Joash	24:25–27	12:19–21
	Jehoahaz		Jehoahaz (Israel)		13:1–9
	Jehoash		Jehoash (Israel)		13:10–13
			Elisha's final prophecy and death		13:14–25
Amaziah		Various	Amaziah (Judah)	25:1–16	14:1–20
			Israel defeats Judah	25:17–24	14:8–14
			Death of Amaziah	25:25–28	14:17–20
Uzziah/Azariah[43]	Jeroboam II	Isaiah, Oded, Jonah	The wars, godly reign and army of Uzziah (Judah)	26:1–15	14:21–29; 15:1–5
			Jeroboam II (Israel)		14:23–29
			Sinful offering of Uzziah	26:16–21	
			Azariah (Judah)		15:1-6
			Death of Uzziah	26:22–23	15:6–7
	Zechariah	Isaiah, Oded	Zechariah (Israel)		15:8–12
	Shallum		Shallum (Israel)		15:13–16
	Menahem		Menahem (Israel)		15:17–22
	Pekahiah		Pekahiah (Israel)		15:23–26
Jotham	Pekah		Pekah (Israel)		15:27–31
			Jotham (Judah)	27:1–9	15:32–38
Ahaz	Hoshea		Israel and Aram (Syria) defeat Ahaz (Judah)	28:1–21	16:1–9
		Isaiah	Ahaz's idolatry and death	28:22–27	16:10–12
			Fall of Israel and explanation		17:1–23
			Resettlement of Israel with foreigners who became the Samaritans		17:24–41

---

43 The same king.

Study 14 ∎

2 Chronicles 10-12 – Imperfect King Rehoboam

The table on pages 67-68 is one that can never be completely correct because there are uncertainties about some of the reigns, co-regencies and other complications[44]. However, it shows the division of the kingdom into two parts, north and south, Israel (or Samaria) and Judah. No doubt, such a rift was required in order to display the differences between the relatively godly[45] southern kingdom and the consistently ungodly northern kingdom. And that is what the Chronicler does, he focuses mainly on the kingdom of Judah, with its kings who are David's and Solomon's descendants. These are the messianic kings, whose job is to prefigure the great Son of David to come in the future (Matthew 1:1). But, first, he deals with the split ...

Read 2 Chronicles 10:1-11:4.

Q1. Why does the Chronicler now focus on what happened to *Rehoboam* and his descendants?

Jeremiah 33:17

2 Chronicles 6:16

Q2. Why do things go so badly wrong for *Rehoboam*?

HIS OWN STUPIDITY   POOR ADVICE   IGNORING GOOD ADVICE

NOT ASKING GOD   SOLOMON'S 'HEAVY YOKE'   GOD'S PROMISE

---

44 There are also apparent difficulties, such as whether to call *Jehoram* king of Israel *Joram* (with the NIV), or to call him *Jehoram* (ESV)– which is obviously confusing because of the contemporary king of Israel having the same name. Happily this is not really a problem in the book of Chronicles, only in 2 Kings. The names are close enough in the original language to be considered variants. See various Bible footnotes on 2 Kings 3:1,6.
45 The word 'relatively' is important.

SOLOMON'S IDOLATRY   JEROBOAM MAKING TROUBLE

1 Kings 11:29-33

2 Chronicles 11:2-4

Read 11:5-17

Q3. Despite God's severe chastisement of *Israel* and *Rehoboam* in splitting the kingdom, what signs of spiritual progress do we see in the southern kingdom (*Judah*)?

11:13   11:16

11:17

Note how many of the twelve tribes this involved (11:16).

Q4. What signs of spiritual degeneration are there already in the northern kingdom (*Israel*)?

11:14   11:15

Read 11:18-23.

Q5. In what ways does *Rehoboam* seem to have learned his lesson and also to have recovered maybe a little of Solomon's wisdom?

11:18

11:23

Q6. What sinister reminders are there in *Rehoboam* of the previous failures of his ancestors?

11:20   Genesis 29:30

The division of the perfect kingdom

2 Samuel 11:2-5   Genesis 37:4

11:21   Deuteronomy 17:17

1 Kings 11:3

Read 12:1-8.

Q7. What cycle do we see repeating itself in these verses?

12:2   Judges 2:19

Q8. How would 12:6-8 prove helpful to the returned exiles in Jerusalem?

See also 12:12.

Read 12:13-16.

Q9. What would seem to be the root causes of *Rehoboam's* calamitous *reign*?

12:13c   12:14

Application

The end of 12:13 attaches great importance to the rôle of motherhood. See also 1 Kings 22:51-53 to see what effect evil king *Ahaziah's mother* had.

Although the wording may seem obscure, King David was clearly blessed by his own mother and wrote about it in Psalm 116:

*16 O L*ORD*, I am your servant;*
  I am your servant, the son of your maidservant [i.e. David's mother]. ESV

The NIV has: *'I serve you just as my mother did'*.

Q10. What can modern mothers learn from these royal mothers?

Discuss:

*'For the hand that rocks the cradle
Is the hand that rules the world.'*[46]

Rehoboam had been set rather a poor example by his father, with his many wives, concubines and subsequent idolatry (1 Kings 11:4). But presumably this was not a major concern for the returned exiles, so the Chronicler does not repeat all the shameful material from 1 Kings 11. He is not whitewashing Solomon, but he does want to avoid discouraging the returned exiles[47].

Furthermore, we see God keeping his promises to his people. This is a two edged sword. For Rehoboam, it meant that his kingdom would be divided as God had promised (10:15). It meant that there was no point trying to resist what God had set in motion (11:4). But for the returned exiles, it meant that there were plenty of promises of blessing to claim as they prayed, repented, laboured, worshipped and waited for the messianic kingdom:

2 Chronicles 7:16... now I have chosen and consecrated this house that my name may be there for ever. My eyes and my heart will be there for all time.

There is also the continual pattern that when his people repent, God forgives, again and again.

The warnings in God's promises should motivate us. The frequent examples of God forgiving should enable us to repent:

Romans 2:4 ... God's kindness is meant to lead you to repentance?

Then, God's promise of an everlasting king, without sin, who has established an everlasting kingdom should keep us continually mining the scriptures for promises to help us to pray, hope, repent and persevere.

But perhaps Rehoboam's major contribution to helping believers through all ages is his warning epitaph:

2 Chronicles 12:14 And he did evil, for he did not set his heart to seek the L ORD.

---

[46] An 1865 poem by William Ross Wallace. The full text can be found here:
https://en.wikisource.org/wiki/The_Hand_That_Rocks_the_Cradle (accessed 2024/01/26).
[47] Who would hardly have been <u>un</u>aware of Solomon's apostasy.

Study 15 ∎

2 Chronicles 13-16 – *The LORD is with you while you are with him ...*

Map showing the divided kingdom after Solomon

The kingdom is well and truly divided[48] by the time the reign of Abijah over Judah starts in 913 BC. In the north, Jeroboam I has been king since 930 BC. His reign is surprisingly long for a king of Israel, 22 years. Abijah's reign in the south is comparatively short for a king of Judah at 3 years – see the table on page 67.

Read 2 Chronicles 13:1-3.

Q1. Despite *Abijah's* short reign, can we predict whether he is likely to prove to be a good king or a bad *king*?

13:2

Q2. Which side seems likely to win the coming *battle*?

13:3

Read 13:4-14:1.

Q3. How do verses 4-12 illustrate Winston Churchill's maxim, *'Jaw, jaw, is always better than to war, war'?*[49]

Q4. Which side did all the 'jawing'?

13:4

Q5. What is the gist of *Abijah's* argument?

Q6. What is the deciding factor in the ensuing battle?

13:8   13:10

13:12   13:15

---
48   The location of the dividing line between the northern and southern kingdoms is uncertain and, in any case, varied over time.
49   *'To jaw-jaw is always better than to war-war'*. speech at the White House, USA, 26 June 1954.

The division of the perfect kingdom   75

Q7. How does *Jeroboam* try to win?

13:13

Q8. What contributions did *Judah* make?

13:10-12

13:15-16   13:18

Read 14:2-6.

Q9. Why was *King Asa* able to do so much *good*?

14:6

Read 15:1-9.

Q10. In what ways do we see *King Asa* to be godly, zealous and even an evangelist?

15:8

15:9

Read 16:2-3,7,10,12

Q11. Though *King Asa* was eventually buried with *honour* (16:14), in what ways do both he and his *grandmother* (Abijah's *mother*!) prove to be a disappointment?

15:16   16:2

16:10   16:12

Application

At first sight, for Abijah, growing up amongst the godly people in Judah and having a mother from Judah seem to give the kingdom a real boost in terms of God's blessing and military success. But after a generation or so, it transpires that the recurrent and besetting sin of idolatry had in fact been a problem for Maacah (15:16) and many others of God's people (15:8). So, whilst things had gone really quite well during Abijah's reign, they started to fall apart during Asa's, in chapter 16. How often do our sins find us out (Numbers 32:23)? How often do they affect subsequent generations? We need to learn from Maacah, her son and grandson that, as the prophet *Azariah* said,

2 Chronicles 15:2 "... The LORD is with you while you are with him. If you seek him, he will be found by you, but if you forsake him, he will forsake you."

Discuss:

All this is hard, requiring faith, effort and sacrifice. But, we have also seen great victories in these chapters:

- Abijah's defeat of Jeroboam through godliness, faith and prayer (13:10-20);
- Asa's defeat of the Cushites (14:8-14, which we may not have read this time);
- Asa's 'evangelistic' campaign which went much further than just the borders of Judah (15:8-9).

But a new thread appears, that of compromise. Sometimes, compromise can be a good thing, but not in the case of Asa allying himself with Baasha of Israel or Ben-Hadad of Aram (Syria; 16:1-2). This becomes a recurring problem for the kings of Judah, and we need to consider how not to repeat their mistakes in our day too.

Discuss:

Homework: The next study covers many chapters, so it is recommended that you read 2 Chronicles 17-21:3 before the next meeting.

Study 16 ■

2 Chronicles 17-21:3 – Jehoshaphat models repentance

After the disappointment that was Asa in his latter years, Jehoshaphat becomes king of Judah in about 872 BC. There seems to have been a period of co-regency with his father, Asa, but Jehoshaphat's reign is roughly contemporary with that of Ahab, king of Israel. They present us with a strongly contrasting pair of kings.

Read 2 Chronicles 17:1-13.

Q1. What kind of king is *Jehoshaphat*?

17:3   17:6

Q2. What was central to the new spiritual climate in *Judah*?

17:7-9

Q3. In what ways did *the* LORD add further blessing despite the slightly sinister wording of 17:3?

17:5   17:10-11

17:12

The Chronicler does not spend much time on the northern kings, but Ahab of Israel is singled out in this ironic and yet sad story.

Read 18:1-19:3.

Q4. What mistake did *Jehoshaphat* make that he may have learned from his father *Asa* (16:7-9)?

18:1

Q5. Do we have a tendency to repeat the mistakes of our forebears?
Discuss:

How can we avoid this?

17:9

Q6. How does *Jehoshaphat* distinguish himself from *Ahab*?

18:6   18:7

Q7. Why does the Chronicler leave the detail in 18:13-16?

Ahab entering the battle with the Arameans (Syrians) in disguise is a classic example of where the Bible is at its most serious when it is at its most humorous!

Q8. Who reveals himself to be behind apparently random[50] actions (18:33)?

Discuss:

18:33

18:27

18:31

One wonders if the prophet *Micaiah* was ever released from prison (18:26).

Read 20:1-13; 23.

---

[50] The Hebrews says that someone '*drew his bow in complete innocence*'. In other words, he was not deliberately aiming at the king of Israel.

The division of the perfect kingdom

Q9. Is there any evidence that *Jehoshaphat* has learned the lesson of the earlier *Ahab* episode?

20:2-3

20:5-6

Q10. What 'arguments' does *Jehoshaphat* use with the LORD (noting the poignancy of v13)?

20:6

20:7

20:8

20:9

20:12

20:13

Q11. What were the results of *Jehoshaphat's* godliness and the LORD'S faithfulness?

20:27   20:28

20:29

Application

And so, like his father Asa, though far from being a perfect king, Jehoshaphat ends up being an evangelist to the nations around him (20:29)! Yet we sometimes feel that we cannot speak up for our Lord because our own lives have let him down. Our sin undermines our confidence. Then we feel guilty for keeping quiet. This spiral needs to be broken.

> **Q12.** How does the story of Jehoshaphat, the tainted evangelist king, help us with our witness-bearing nowadays?
>
> **Discuss:**

Once again, we see the problem of compromising with the ungodly, highlighted this time by the prophet *Hanani*[51]:

2 Chronicles 19:2 ... "Should you help the wicked and love those who hate the Lord? Because of this, wrath has gone out against you from the LORD."

Yet, Jehoshaphat clearly repents of allying himself with Ahab, so the final verdict on his leadership was that he was a good king (20:32). Once again, his mother seems to be mentioned as a factor in his godliness (20:31).

How is it possible for a sinful, foolish and comprising king like Jehoshaphat to be declared a good king in the end? How was Jehoshaphat's sin atoned for? Is he really any different from us?

Homework: Dig out one or two family trees of group members for next time ...

---

51   But spoken by his *son, Jehu*.

The division of the perfect kingdom

Study 17 ■

2 Chronicles 21:4-24:27 – Families!

King Jehoram (848 – 841 BC) is a bit of a shock after Jehoshaphat. But, 21:3 should have set alarm bells ringing.

Read 2 Chronicles 21:4-7.

Q1. What are the signs that this *king* is not going to last long?

21:4   21:5

21:6   21:6   21:6

Q2. What great covenant is continued in 21:7?

1 Chronicles 17:11-14

Q3. What signs do we see from the rest of the chapter that God was really not pleased with *Jehoram*. See the map on page 73. Note where *Jehoram* was buried.

21:8   21:10

21:12-15 (see *Tishbe* on map (1 Kings 17:1))

21:16[52]   21:18

21:20[53]   21:20

---
52 Note the reversal of 2 Chronicles 17:11 in Jehoshaphat's time.
53 Notice/enjoy the unique epitaph.

The Perfect Kingdom?

Read 22:1-9.

Q4. What signs are there that *Ahaziah* is not going to prove to be a good king? See the map on page 73.

22:1   22:2

22:2   22:3

22:4   22:5

Q5. Who was *Ahaziah's* real enemy?

HIS MOTHER   KING AHAB'S DYNASTY   KING HAZAEL

KING JORAM   JEHU SON OF NIMSHI   GOD

Q6. Is there any encouragement in the passage that the LORD has remembered his covenant promises to King David?

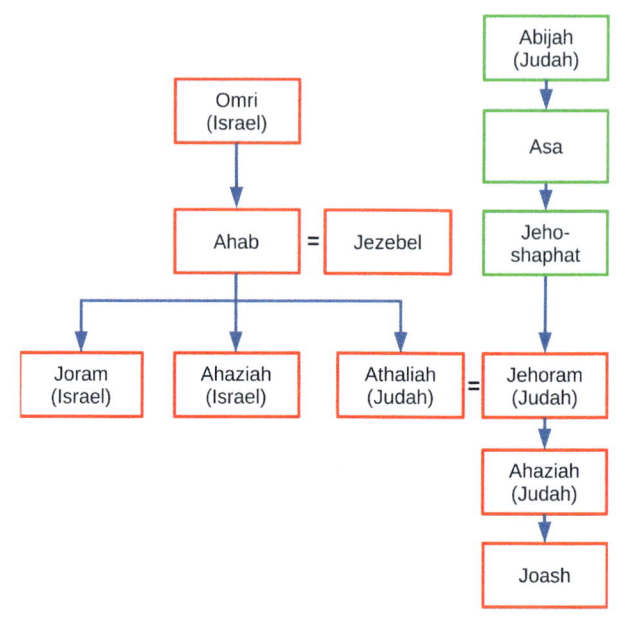

Evil tracing its way down from Omri to Joash with help from Jezebel and Athaliah

Family trees can tell you a lot about where you came from. Sadly, they can sometimes predict what we will tend to be like as well. There is no more scary a family tree than the one connecting Omri king of Israel to Joash[54] king of Judah.

Q7. How did the LORD act in order to keep his promise to King David? Notice the significance of where *Joash* was hidden. See Exodus 2:1-10 for a similar set of providences.

22:11

Read 23:1-3; 14-15; 24:1-2

> **Q8.** Does God ever need his people's help to keep his promises?
> **Discuss:**
> 23:3
>
> 23:14-15
>
> 24:2

Read 24:17-22;25.
It would seem as if all that effort to hide *Joash* in the *temple*, proclaim him *king*, guard and guide him, were all wasted.

Application

The problem, of course, was not God's providence in saving Joash, nor Jehoiada's careful training of a mere boy king (24:1), nor can the blame be laid completely at the feet of the *princes* ESV *(officials* NIV*) of Judah* (24:17-18). The underlying issue was a heart attitude. The heart attitude that King David had (Acts 13:22) was not transmitted automatically to his heir King Joash. He was the Davidic king in biology but not in his heart, so:

2 Chronicles 24:25 ... he died, and they buried him in the city of David, but they did not bury him in the tombs of the kings.

---

[54] Spoiler alert: The boy king, Joash started off well.

It is possible, like Ahaziah, to have so many enemies that a person does not notice who is main enemy is.

Q9. So, was the LORD unfaithful? Did *he* fail to keep his promises?

7:17-18

24:20

Q10. What tools do we have at our disposal to prevent such a "bitter root" (Deuteronomy 29:18) from growing amongst us?

Hebrews 12:11-15

Jude 20-23

2 Peter 1:10

1 John 5:13-17

Mark 4:1-20

Hebrews 10:23-25

Romans 8:15-17

Study 18 ■

2 Chronicles 25-28 – How good is your king?

There has been a lot of controversy recently about assigning single or double-word assessment categories to individual schools, such as 'Outstanding' or 'Requires Improvement'. The kings in these sections go from outstanding to downright pagan.

OFSTED SCHOOL RATINGS
Outstanding
Good
Requires Improvement
Inadequate

Scan the passages and assign Ofsted ratings to each of them.

2 CHRONICLES	KING/QUEEN	OFSTED SCHOOL RATING
17-20	*Jehoshaphat*[55]	
21:4-20	*Jehoram*[55]	
22:1-9	*Ahaziah*[55]	
22:10-23:21	*Athaliah*[55]	
24	*Joash*[55]	
25	*Amaziah*	
26	*Uzziah (Azariah)*	
27	*Jotham*	
28	*Ahaz*	

The following questions may help to winkle out the verdicts.

---
55 From previous study.

Read 25:1-8.

Q1. How do the following passages incline towards giving *King Amaziah* an 'Outstanding'?

25:1   25:3

25:4   25:8

Q2. How might the following passage make you want to downgrade *King Amaziah's* assessment?

25:2

Remember that the Chronicler is concerned with 'all *Israel*' and that many *Ephraimites* had joined with Judah and Benjamin.

25:7

25:14-15   25:20-22

Read 26:1-8.

Q3. How would you assess *King Uzziah* at first?

26:2   26:3

26:3   26:4

26:5   26:7-8

Q4. How did *King Uzziah* blot his copy book?

26:16   26:20

The division of the perfect kingdom

Recall how leprosy in scripture often symbolises sin (Leviticus 13-14).

Read 27:1-9.

Q5. Assess *King Jotham* in the same ways as previously?

27:1	27:2
27:2	27:2
27:5	27:6
27:9	

Read 28:1-9.

Q6. Assess *King Ahaz* in the same ways as previously?

28:1	28:2
28:3	28:5
28:27	

Q7. How did *King Ahaz'* great evil affect others?

28:3	28:5
28:8	

Ahaz reigned from roughly 735 to 715 BC. During this period, the northern kingdom had been going from bad to worse and were being sent into captivity in a number of stages:

ASSYRIAN DEPORTATIONS OF ISRAEL		
734-732 BC	Tiglath-Pileser III invaded Israel.	Reuben, Gad, and the half-tribe of Manasseh were deported to Assyria and replaced with people from other countries.
725-722 BC	Shalmaneser V conquered Israel and laid siege to Samaria.	Most of the Israelite population deported to Assyria.
722 BC	Samaria, the capital city, fell.	Deported Israelites scattered throughout Assyrian empire, and replaced by foreigners.[56]

Read 28:9-15.

Q8. What were the key ingredients of God's grace to the captured people from Judah?

28:9   28:12

28:15   Genesis 3:11,21

28:19

Read 28:22-25.

Q9. What are the key elements that would eventually lead to Judah also being exiled?

28:22   28:23 (note '*all Israel*')

28:24   28:25

Application

After some good kings, and some who needed improvement, Ahaz's decent into total paganism mirrored what was going on in the northern kingdom. He must have seen God deporting the tribes of Israel and yet persisted in his unrepentance (28:22). Even though he and his people were greatly humbled (28:19) before Israel and the Assyrians he goes even further afield to find some gods who will help him (28:23): anything but turn back to his own God (28:22), *the God of his fathers* (28:25).

---

[56] This is the origin of the 'Samaritans' and is explained in 2 Kings 17:24-41.

The division of the perfect kingdom

Do we ever persist in sin? Do we continue despite getting the feeling that God may be chastising us? What we do next is the critical thing. Ahaz went deeper into sin, taking his family and his people with him. His predecessors had often repented; for example, Jehoshaphat decided to depend only on the LORD. But, since him, the kings of Judah had forgotten how to repent. We must make sure that we do stubbornly soldier on in unrepentance, learn to 'keep short accounts with God', confess freely, turn back quickly, find forgiveness, peace and joy daily and weekly, helping others to do the same.

Hebrews 12:5 And have you forgotten the exhortation that addresses you as sons?

   "My son, do not regard lightly the discipline of the Lord,
   nor be weary when reproved by him.
⁶ For the Lord disciplines the one he loves,
 and chastises every son whom he receives."

Think, too, about how easily we formed assessments of these four kings of Judah, judging them by our human categories.

Q10. How will God judge us on the day of judgement?

John 5:27-29   Revelation 20:13

Revelation 7:9-14   Revelation 3:5

These kings of Judah failed to set us a good example. They also failed to live as 'types' of the ultimate son of David, King Jesus. Furthermore, the people of Judah were federally and legally 'in'[57] their kings who often let them down, bringing disaster on all of the people, not just on themselves (28:3-8). We must make sure that we are 'in Christ', *in* his *book of life*, thereby bringing blessing to ourselves and others around us:

Romans 8:1 There is therefore now no condemnation for those who are in Christ [i.e. the one anointed king] *Jesus.*

---

[57] To understand this short word, 'in', study the book of Ephesians, noting all the uses of that word.

5 The continuation of the perfect kingdom?

King	Prophet/ Prophetess	About	2 Chronicles	2 Kings
Hezekiah	Isaiah	Hezekiah cleanses the temple	29:1–19	18:1–8
	Isaiah, David (previously)	Hezekiah restores temple worship	29:20–36	
		Hezekiah restores Passover	30:1–27	
		Hezekiah destroys idols, organizes priests	31:1–21	
	Isaiah, others	Fall of Israel explained		18:9–12
		Assyria (Sennacherib) captures most of Judah	32:1–23	18:13–19:37
		Hezekiah's illness and restoration	32:24–26	20:1–11
		Hezekiah's wealth and foolish pride; death	32:27–33	20:12–21
Manasseh		Manasseh's evil reign	33:1–9	21:1–18
		Manasseh's repentance	33:10–20	
Amon		Amon's evil reign	33:21–25	21:19–26
Josiah	Huldah the prophetess	Josiah's early reforms; repairs the temple	34:1–13	22:1–7
		Book of the Law found; Josiah's reforms	34:14–33	22:8–23:20
		Passover celebrated	35:1–19	23:21–27
		Death of Josiah	35:20–27	23:28–30
Jehoahaz		Jehoahaz	36:1–3	23:31–33
Jehoiakim		Jehoiakim	36:4–8	23:34–24:7
Jehoiachin		Jehoiachin and his Babylonian (Chaldean[58]) captivity	36:9–10	24:8–17
Zedekiah	Jeremiah	Zedekiah and the destruction of Jerusalem	36:11–21	24:18–25:21
		Remnant flees to Egypt (taking Jeremiah)		25:22–26
Jehoiachin		Jehoiachin released		25:27–30
Cyrus the Medo-Persian emperor		Proclamation by Cyrus	36:22–23	

Did the deportation of all the idolatrous northern tribes then result in a perfect, southern, kingdom of God, with godly messianic kings who were sons of David both biologically and spiritually? These remaining studies will reveal all ...

---

[58] The names Babylon and Chaldea are largely interchangeable, the latter being simply the Greek for Babylon.

Study 19 ■

2 Chronicles 29-32 – Hezekiah, a truly Christlike king

After that last ungodly batch of kings of Judah, no doubt the returned exiles breathed a sigh of relief to read about the next king, Hezekiah (715 BC to 686 BC). But first, we need to appreciate the scale of devastation that has been going on (see map on page 94).

The northern kingdom, previously known as Israel, Samaria or even Ephraim, has basically gone into exile in Assyria. They are replaced by foreigners (2 Kings 17:24-41), some of whose descendants become the *Samaritans* of Jesus' day (John 4:22).

Read 2 Chronicles 29:1-11.

Q1. What are the indicators in the text of what kind of king *Hezekiah* is going to be?

29:1   29:1

29:3   29:4-11

Given what *Hezekiah's* father had been like, imagine how important the rôle of his *mother Abijah* (29:1) must have been! It also seems significant that she (a female) was named after a genuinely godly (male) king from 200 years previously. Often, the Chronicler's lessons are not overtly spelled out. Notice how he calls Jerusalem *the City of David* in 32:5.[59]

Cast an eye over 29:3 to 29:27. These verses are not in Kings.

Q2. Looking at this material, why do you suppose the Chronicler has included it for the benefit of the returned exiles perhaps 265 years later?

29:1   29:16

---
59 The *Millo* (ESV) is probably another defensive wall.

29:19   29:20-24

29:25-26

Map showing the northern kingdom taken into exile by Tiglath-Pileser III of Assyria, then Shalmaneser V and Sargon II

The continuation of the perfect kingdom?

Q3. How does *Hezekiah* demonstrate evangelistic zeal? Consult the map on page 94.

30:5   30:10-11

Q4. What is the gist of *Hezekiah's letter* in 30:6-9?

Q5. How must *Hezekiah* have felt in 32:1 (701 BC)? Bear in mind that at this point *Hezekiah* is only really king over Jerusalem and the immediately surrounding area. Most of *Judah* has been lost! See 32:9 and *Lachish* on the map.

Read and enjoy the whole story in 32:1-23.

Q6. How does *Hezekiah* combine both practical and spiritual leadership in 32:2-8?

32:2-6

32:7-8

Q7. What did *Sennacherib* clearly misunderstand? *Hezekiah* did not have this problem (32:8)!

32:10-15

Q8. How do *Sennacherib* and his messengers really seal their own fate?

32:16   32:17

32:17

Q9. How many verses does it take *the* LORD to sort out *Sennacherib*?

Application

Interestingly, it actually took 20 years until two of *Sennacherib's sons* assassinated him (681 BC) *in the temple his god*. Both *Sennacherib* and the nameless[60] godlet who could not save him were humiliated! But, it took 20 years. That should teach us lessons about patience, and about waiting for God's final deliverance from all our enemies.

It seems a miracle that Hezekiah should be such a good king when his father had been a downright pagan. And, no doubt, it was, because even with a godly upbringing from his mother a regenerating work in his heart by God the Holy Spirit was needed in his day just as much as it is in ours! But his heart is exposed as loving and trusting the LORD in his urging of the people to repentance, and in his trusting stand against Sennacherib.

Perhaps it is David and Hezekiah who best model the kingship of the Lord Jesus Christ? Like Jesus, they were both pure in heart. Like Jesus will, they both saw eventual victory despite great struggles with the enemies of God's people (Luke 20:41-44). Unlike Jesus, they both had significant flaws, but in the Bible the 'type' is never allowed to outshine the real thing. We must emulate David and Hezekiah, but Jesus is the only king we should worship.

When we do manage to get our 'ducks in a row' – quiet time (tick), Bible study (tick), set kids a good example (tick), love spouse (tick), help neighbour (tick), share with someone about Jesus (tick), get everyone to church to start the new week well (tick) etc., we feel we have had a good week and will surely start the next one under God's blessing.

> **Q10.** But, how do we feel when the equivalent of Sennacherib greets us on Monday morning?
>
> **Discuss:**

You did enjoy reading chapter 32, didn't you? If you are on the LORD'S side, joy should always be there somewhere. Whilst we may be sad about the fate of those who set themselves up against our God, scripture is clear:

1 Thessalonians 5:16 Rejoice always, [17] pray without ceasing, [18] give thanks in all circumstances; for this is the will of God in Christ Jesus for you.

But notice, once again, that Hezekiah is not whitewashed in the final section from 32:24-26.

---

60 The god is named in Isaiah 37:38.

Study 20 ■

2 Chronicles 33 – Manasseh: Amazing Grace!

When John Newton wrote the hymn *Amazing Grace*, it was from his own perspective as a former slave trader and general reprobate. It is fascinating to see how it was associated in his Olney Hymns of 1779 with the book of 1 Chronicles.

Some versions of the hymn make it read as if it was the *'sweet ... sound'* that *'saved the wretch like me'*. But Newton was clear: It was 'grace'.

King Manasseh (697 BC to 642 BC) of Judah was a much greater reprobate, making John Newton look like a part-time amateur! And yet, he discovered the same amazing grace.

Sing *Amazing Grace* together[61].

Read 2 Chronicles 33:1-11, 20.

Q1. Based on your knowledge of previous kings, what details does the Chronicler omit from verse 1?

Q2. What is unusual about verse 20?

---
61   Noting, of course, that the letter 'f' is actually an 's', e.g. *the sun forbear to shine*, verse 6, line 2.

List *King Manasseh's* sins.

33:2   33:3

33:3   33:3

33:4   33:5

33:6   33:6

33:7   33:9

33:10

There is also a Jewish tradition[62] that King Manasseh executed the prophet Isaiah.

Q3. Why do you think the Chronicler works into *Manasseh's* list of sins reminders about *God's law*, *God's* gracious acts, and even *Hezekiah's* deeds?

33:2

33:3

33:4

33:7

33:8

---
62 Talmud, Sanhedrin 103b.

33:10

And so, *Manasseh* who had behaved like the *people* of the northern kingdom and the various pagans around is invaded, conquered and imprisoned by the same foreign foe, the *Assyrians* in perhaps 648 BC.

Q4. What surprising foretaste does *the* LORD give *Manasseh*?[63] This may have been quite poignant for the returned exiles in *Jerusalem*.

33:11

Q5. What major addition does the Chronicler make compared with the writer of 2 Kings? See the table on page 91 or look through 2 Kings 21:10-18.

Read 33:12-20.

Q6. Are you now glad that we have Chronicles in addition to Kings?

Q7. In what senses was *the* LORD *Manasseh's God*? Compare this verse with the parables in Luke 15.

33:12

Q8. How does the Chronicler summarise *Manasseh's* conversion experience in a way that would have been most encouraging to the returned exiles (and to us!)?

33:13   33:13

Q9. How can we be sure that *Manasseh's* conversion was genuine[64]?

33:14   33:15

---
63 In addition to the *hook(s)* and the *bronze shackles*.
64 I am writing this a couple of days after an Afghan 'convert' to Christianity used a noxious substance to mutilate some women and children in Clapham, London, UK.

33:16   33:17(!)

Matthew 12:33

Q10. How could the returned exiles check that the Chronicler was telling the truth? It does all seem rather amazing.

33:18-19

Q11. Do we perhaps get an indication that the people of Israel were less forgiving than *the* LORD?

33:20

Read 33:21-25.

Q12. What was the critical difference between *Amon* and his *father Manasseh*?

33:23   1 Peter 5:5-6

Application

My late father[65] described the 2 Chronicles 33 version of Manasseh's reign as the most encouraging chapter in the Bible.

Discuss:

Surely, if God could, and did, save Manasseh, he can save anyone. We should therefore never give up praying for our own reprobates, prodigals etc.

---
65   John D. Legg (1936 - 2023)

John Knox[66], the Scottish reformer, wrote this prayer for *'the Obstinate or Unrepentant'* in his 1564 – 1643 Liturgy. You may like to make use of it, if it helps.

> *Lord, you alone can change and soften the hearts of the proud and impenitent. You, by the voice of the prophet Nathan, awakened King David from his deadly complacency. You, without the help of any prophet, overcame the pride of King Manasseh in prison, after he had shed the blood of your servants, and had filled Jerusalem with all kinds of iniquity. You turned the heart of the apostle Peter by a single look from your dear Son our Lord Jesus Christ, after fear had led Peter to curse himself and openly disown him.*
>
> *Lord, your mercies are without measure and endure for ever. After much long effort, we therefore bring this obstinate and unrepentant person to you, earnestly desiring that you, the Father of Mercies, will pierce his [or her] heart with the fear of your judgement, that he [or she] may begin to understand that he [or she] is provoking you to wrath and indignation against himself [or herself].*
>
> *Open his eyes that he may see how fearful and terrible a thing it is to fall into your hands. And, thereafter, soften his heart by the working of your Holy Spirit that he [or she] may give to you that honour and obedience commanded in your holy word.*
>
> *We mourn for his [or her] rebellion and long that he [or she] subject himself [or herself] to the legitimate ordinances of your church and avoid the fearful vengeance that will most assuredly fall on all the disobedient. In the name of our sovereign master, Jesus Christ, we call for your gracious action. Amen.*[67]

---

66 https://en.wikipedia.org/wiki/John_Knox. Accessed 2023/02/3.
67 Taken from a slightly modernised version in my *Reformed Evangelical Ministry Resources, Orders of Service, Prayers, Confessions, Doxologies, Blessings, Catechisms*, 3.12, Covenant Books UK, 2023. https://www.amazon.co.uk/dp/B0C5221743. The original is harder-going, but available here: https://archive.org/details/liturgyjohnknox00knoxuoft. Accessed 2024/02/03.

Study 21 ■

2 Chronicles 34-35 – Josiah delays disaster

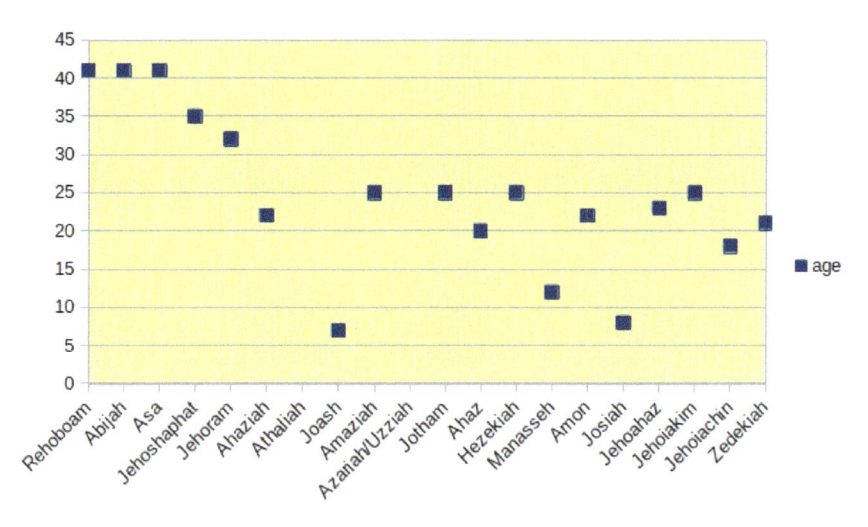

Accession Ages of the Kings of Judah

After the shocking roller-coaster of King Manasseh's reign, what do you notice about the next king, Josiah?

Read 2 Chronicles 34:1-8.

Q1. Given 33:23 and 34:1, what is remarkable about *Josiah* and his *reign*?

34:2   34:3

34:6 (see map on page 94)

34:33 (looking ahead)

Q2. But how long did it take him to get around to a certain really important thing?

34:8

Read 34:14-22.

Q3. What other vital ingredient had been omitted from an otherwise godly rule?

34:14   34:21

34:22

Q4. Whose fault was it that these important matters had been ignored, and who then took responsibility?

34:9   34:14-15

34:20

It had taken 18 years to rediscover the word of *God*, even though it was available, *in Jerusalem* (Deuteronomy 30:11-14), from several different sources!

Read what the *prophetess* Huldah said in 34:23-28.

Q5. What did *Josiah* have in common with *Manasseh* (not with *Amon*), and what was the corresponding blessing from the LORD?

33:23   34:27

34:28

Read 35:1, 16-19, 20-23

Q6. How might *Josiah's* immediate obedience in this way have been a great encouragement to the returned exiles in Jerusalem 160 or so years later?

The continuation of the perfect kingdom?

Q7. Having tried so zealously to obey the word of God, albeit somewhat late, what final mistake does *Josiah* make?

34:21   34:22

2 Chronicles 18:33 (Review answer to Q8 on page 78.)

Application

The word of God has historically come to his people from numerous directions – prophets, kings, priests, apostles etc., and even from a pagan pharaoh (34:22).

Q8. What sources of God's word might we accidentally ignore nowadays?

Discuss:

We have seen Josiah evangelistic zeal even though he was inadequately versed in God's law. He sets us a magnificent example, especially for one from such a dire background, and for one who became king so young. No wonder Christians like to name their sons Josiah! There are not so many Manassehs, Amons, Ahabs and Jezebels around[68].

Nevertheless, Josiah's reign was spoiled by it not being informed directly by the law of God and by the state of the derelict temple in Jerusalem.

---
[68] In fact, no-one in the UK had been name Ahab or Jezebel this century, when I enquired in around 2014.

Q9. How should the word of *God*, the *temple (the house of the* LORD*)*, *Hilkiah the high priest*, *Shaphan the secretary*, and *Josiah the king* all have related to each other in a spiritually healthy manner?

Deuteronomy 17:18

How can we learn from their mistakes for modern church life?

Discuss:

Study 22 ■

2 Chronicles 36:1-23 – The end of the perfect kingdom?

> *Progress, far from consisting in change, depends on retentiveness. When change is absolute there remains no being to improve and no direction is set for possible improvement: and when experience is not retained, as among savages, infancy is perpetual. Those who cannot remember the past are condemned to repeat it.*[69] – George Santyana

We come now to the end of the 'perfect kingdom'. Of course, a perfect kingdom would never end, and we discover that this was not really the perfect kingdom itself but a 'type' of it. Certainly it was God's kingdom on earth, but a very limited version. The best version was brought in by King Jesus (Mark 1:15), and even that has not yet been completely fulfilled yet.

Nevertheless, God's first kingdom was dissolved at a huge cost and with immense pain, suffering, sin and complexity (see Jeremiah 39-45 and the relevant parts of 2 Kings referred to in the table on page 91), so we should not simply skip to the NT without first taking the trouble to learn from the past[69]. The returned exiles who were the Chronicler's first readers did not need to re-read *what* happened in the end, but they did need a reminder of *why* it all happened (2 Chronicles 36:15-21).

Chapter 36 covers from 609 to 538 BC – the date of Cyrus the Medo-Persian emperor's decree sending the exiles back to Jerusalem. This period of 71 years is very similar to the 70 years of exile prophesied by Jeremiah, if it is assumed to be counting from the first deportations[70] of Judah in 605 BC (~67 years). The first exiles began to return with Sheshbazzar[71] (Ezra 1:8) in around 537 BC (~68 years), making the 70 years in Jeremiah 25:11 presumably a gracious, round number.

---

[69] Spanish-American philosopher George Santyana, *The Life of Reason* (1905-1906), https://www.gutenberg.org/files/15000/15000-h/15000-h.htm, accessed 2024/02/12.
[70] It is possible that the very first deportations happened as early as 608 BC. This would certainly be arithmetically convenient!
[71] Who may be the same man as Zerubbabel, according to Josephus (*Antiquities* 11.1.3). He laid the second temple's foundation stone in 536 BC.

Read 2 Chronicles 36:1-14.

Draw a family tree of the 'last' five kings of Judah before the exile.

'Last' Five Judean Kings	
Josiah	(640-609 BC)
Jehoahaz	(609 BC)
Jehoiakim (Eliakim)	(609-598 BC)
Jehoiachin	(598-597 BC)
Zedekiah	(597-586 BC)

Q1. Deduce whether each was a good or bad king and annotate the tree.

Family Tree of 'Last' 5 Kings of Judah
Josiah (GOOD)

Q2. What signs of the LORD's displeasure can you pick up from the passage?

36:2   36:3

36:4   36:5

36:6-7   36:9

The change of name in 36:4 shows the power over Judah exerted by Pharaoh Neco (609 BC). The two names involved have essentially the same ironic meaning 'God will establish'.[72]

---
[72] But from the returned exiles' perspective, this may actually have been encouraging.

The continuation of the perfect kingdom?

Q3. In what ways did things get even worse under Zedekiah?

36:12

36:13

36:14

Read 36:15-19.[58]

Q4. What features of this passage do you find particularly upsetting?
Discuss:

Read the parable of the tenants in Matthew 21:33-45.

Q5. In what ways is the parable similar to 2 Chronicles 36:15-19?

Q6. In what ways is the parable far worse than 2 Chronicles 26:15-19.

Read 36:20-23.

In the parable of the tenants, the fate of the evil tenants is absolutely final (Matthew 21:41-43).

Q7. How does the Chronicler show the situation in 2 Chronicles 36 to be less 'final' and not the absolute end for the kingdom?

36:20   36:21

36:23

Q8. What clues are there that the Lord God is in control?

36:21   36:22

36:23   36:23

Application

How the returned exiles in Jerusalem would have treasured your answers to those last two questions. Their inadequate temple and rickety city walls were saying that God had abandoned them; the temple hadn't even got the ark of the covenant inside it, the symbol of God's presence. But, the encouraging note on which Chronicles ends could only have warmed their hearts.

In the same way, we can hear and see people in the media talking about a post-Christian age and the secular age in which live as if God had given up on his kingdom. How important it is to use scripture as a spiritual and kingdom barometer and not the BBC!

Similarly, the exiles would have looked around and seen each other in poverty, struggling to survive in a world controlled by their slave masters and enemies. How they needed to know that God was in control – and not just any old pagan god like Baal or Ashtoreth, but their own God, the true God, the Lord, the God of their ancestors. We too can trace our spiritual lineage right back through all the Hebrew part of the Bible to Abraham and even to before him. The people of God have formed a kingdom since the time of Adam really. That kingdom has not always gone too well, but it has always had a powerful backer. In 450 BC, it no longer had an obvious king, but the Lord was still their king.

The returned exiles need to *put first the kingdom of God and his righteousness* (Matthew 6:33) if they were going to succeed with keeping God's kingdom going until the Messiah would come and save them. They had to prioritise what *God* had ordained: the *house of God* (*temple*); its worship; its teaching; kingdom holiness; the promised *land* and its *Sabbaths*; the city of God; the people of God.

> **Q9.** What priorities do we need to have in God's kingdom nowadays as we wait for the King's second coming?
>
> **Discuss:**
>
> Matthew 6:33
>
> 2 Peter 3:11-12

This study has been kept fairly short[73] to allow you extra time to read the final chapter that follows ...

---

73 Unless you spent too long drawing the family tree!

6 Whatever happened to the perfect kingdom?

Map of Roman Empire, AD 210 — PROVINCIAE IMPERII ROMANORUM

The map above shows the Roman Empire in 210 AD. At the right hand end, the province of 'Syria-Palestina' can be clearly seen. Such a map begs the question, 'Where is the perfect kingdom of God after Bible times?' The Bible was certainly complete by 100 AD. Although it has sometimes been attempted, nothing has been added to the completed canon since the first century. And yet the biblical geography is still there. It may have different names; descendants of the biblical people still live there. But, where is God's kingdom? Where did the King say it would be?

Luke 17:20 Being asked by the Pharisees when the kingdom of God would come, he answered them, "The kingdom of God is not coming with signs to be observed,²¹ nor will they say, 'Look, here it is!' or 'There!' for behold, the kingdom of God is in the midst of you." [or within you, ESV margin]

If we could zoom into the map, we would still not be able to see the actual kingdom of God, because it is inside and made up of all its people, including those who have died and gone to heaven. But, we could see God's kingdom spreading all across the Roman Empire and, from there, *to the ends of the earth* (Acts 1:8).

When the king returns, he will judge by what is in people's hearts (Isaiah 11:3) and will recreate the heavens and earth, which will become the final kingdom of God. The book (*scroll*) of Revelation describes the completed kingdom in terms of many of the concepts in Chronicles. Jesus is the *offspring*/seed/*son of David*; the *holy city* of Jerusalem is there; God's people have a *share*, an inheritance, in the *city* of God:

Revelation 22:16 "I, Jesus... am the Root and the Offspring of David ..."
... [19] And if anyone takes words away from this scroll of prophecy, God will take away from that person any share in the tree of life and in the Holy City, which are described in this scroll.

It is good to remind ourselves that we have not been studying mere stories, but actual history – see the photograph.

In Chronicles, the kingdom of God seems to start off physically and geographically in the time of the davidic kings, then the final *Son of David* (Luke 18:38) comes for the first time and refines it into a spiritual kingdom (Matthew 12:28; Romans 14:17). When he comes the second time he will recreate it all into a combined spiritual and physical kingdom with the new earth (Revelation 21:1) making up the geography, so the final state will be in every way superior, and glorifying to God. In the meantime, we must keep working and keep praying ...

Clay tablet. The Akkadian cuneiform inscription lists certain rations and mentions the name of Jeconiah (Jehoiachin), King of Judah and the Babylonian captivity. From Babylon, Iraq. Neo-Babylonian period, reign of Nebuchadnezzar II, c. 580 BC. Vorderasiatisches Museum, Berlin. Photo: Osama Shukir Muhammed Amin FRCP (Glasgow), Creative Commons Attribution-Share Alike 4.0 International licence.

Matthew 6:10 your kingdom come, your will be done, on earth as it is in heaven.

Appendix A – The Hebrew Bible (Tanak)

\multicolumn{4}{c}{HEBREW BIBLE (TANAK) [74]}			
DIVISION	**SUB-DIVISION**	**MODERN WESTERN NAME** (TRANSLITERATED HEBREW NAME)	**% OF TANAK**
TORAH (LAW):	**BOOK OF MOSES:**	Genesis (Bereshit)	6.3%
		Exodus (Shemot)	5.1%
		Leviticus (Vayikra)	3.9%
		Numbers (Bamidbar)	5.2%
		Deuteronomy (Devarim)	4.5%
NEVI'IM (PROPHETS):	**FORMER PROPHETS:**	Joshua (Yehoshua)	3.0%
		Judges (Shoftim)	3.0%
		Samuel (Shmuel)	7.3%
		Kings (Melachim)	7.8%
	LATTER PROPHETS:	Isaiah (Yeshayahu)	6.2%
		Jeremiah (Yirmiyahu)	6.9%
		Ezekiel (Yechezkel)	6.4%
		The Twelve Minor Prophets (Trei Asar): (4.9%)	
		- Hosea (Hoshea)	0.9%
		- Joel (Yoel)	0.3%
		- Amos (Amos)	0.7%
		- Obadiah (Ovadiah)	0.1%
		- Jonah (Yonah)	0.2%
		- Micah (Micha)	0.5%
		- Nahum (Nachum)	0.2%
		- Habakkuk (Chavakuk)	0.2%
		- Zephaniah (Tzefanya)	0.3%
		- Haggai (Chaggai)	0.2%
		- Zechariah (Zechariah)	1.0%
		- Malachi (Malachi)	0.3%
KETUVIM (WRITINGS):	**THE SCROLLS:**	Psalms (Tehillim)	7.6%
		Proverbs (Mishlei)	2.6%
		Job (Iyov)	3.1%
		Song of Songs (Shir Hashirim)	0.5%
		Ruth (Rut)	0.4%
		Lamentations (Eichah)	0.6%
		Ecclesiastes (Kohelet)	0.9%
		Esther (Megillat Esther)	0.9%
		Daniel (Daniel)	1.9%
		Ezra-Nehemiah:	3.0%
		Chronicles (Divrei Hayamim)	8.0%

---

[74] Hebrew canon of 2nd C AD, with Chronicles having been entered last in 4th C BC.

General Index

450 BC 8, 9, 10, 38, 110
536 BC 107
586 BC 7, 8, 9, 10, 61, 64, 108
605 BC 107
681 BC 96
70 AD 61
70 years 7, 8, 64, 107
701 BC 95
959 BC 63, 64
ABANDON 52
Abijah 8, 67, 74, 75, 76, 93
Abimelech 12, 13
Abishag 17
Abner 17
Abraham 110
Absalom 17, 36
Accession Ages, Kings' 103
Adam 7, 8, 12, 13, 16, 110
Additions 10
Adonijah 17
Adultery 10, 36
Agricultural themes 32
Ahab 8, 67, 77, 78, 79, 80, 82, 105
Ahaz 8, 68, 85, 87, 88, 89
Ahaziah 8, 67, 68, 71, 82, 84, 85
Ahijah 17, 48, 67
Ahijah the Shilonite 48
Altar 62
Amaziah 68, 85, 86
Amminadab 12
Ammon 67
Ammonites 17, 37, 38
Amnon 17, 36
Amon 8, 91, 100, 104, 105
Apostasy 8, 17
Apostles 49, 105
Arabia 68
Aram 68, 76
Arameans 17, 42, 78
Araunah 41

Arguing with God 28
Ark 17, 23, 24, 25, 26, 29, 31, 43, 60, 63, 66, 110
Army 17, 42, 48, 51, 68
Asa 8, 67, 75, 76, 77, 78, 79
Ashtoreth 110
Assyria 88, 91, 93, 94, 99
Athaliah 68, 85
Atonement 29, 39, 40, 41, 80
Authority 47, 48
Axe head 68
Azariah 67, 68, 76
Baal 110
Baasha 67, 76
Babylon 7, 9, 11, 38
Babylonian 8, 9, 91
Balaam 12
Barnabas 49
Bathsheba 17
Battle 16, 36, 37, 74, 78
Ben-Hadad 67, 68, 76
Benedictions 46
Benjamin 20, 86
Beth-Shemeth 23
Bethlehem 20
Bible Study 3, 96
Bible Study Guides 3
Blessing ... 16, 23, 26, 33, 46, 55, 72, 76, 77, 89, 96, 104
Boaz 12
Book of life 89
Book of Moses 115
Book of the Law 91
Building .. 7, 8, 13, 17, 25, 29, 30, 32, 33, 36, 41, 43, 44, 45, 51, 53, 56, 59, 61, 62
Burnt offerings 29, 55, 63
Canon, of scripture 113
Celebration 21
Census 17
Ceremony 40

Chaldean 91
Chariots of fire 68
Chastisement 8, 17, 37, 70, 89
Chastisements 37
Christians . .9, 10, 21, 34, 37, 47, 49, 61, 105
Church. 3, 16, 21, 29, 45, 48, 58, 62, 96, 101, 106
Circumstances 16, 61, 96
City of David 23
City of David 93
City of God 111, 114
Co-regencies 69, 77
COMMANDS 52
Compromise 76
Concern 9, 52, 53, 72
Concubines 72
Contradictions 42, 56
Cornerstone 45
Coronation 8, 17, 21
Coup 36
Covenant ... 1, 2, 3, 9, 17, 23, 25, 31, 34, 43, 44, 47, 48, 49, 55, 60, 63, 66, 81, 82, 110
Covenant Books UK 1, 2
Covenant representative 47, 48
Creation 13
Creative Commons 2
Cross, the 34, 38, 41
Curses 9
Cushites 76
Cyprus 49
Cyrus 7, 8, 91, 107
David ... 1, 2, 3, 8, 10, 11, 14, 17, 19, 20, 21, 22, 23, 24, 25, 26, 27, 29, 31, 32, 33, 34, 36, 37, 38, 39, 40, 41, 42, 43, 44, 45, 47, 48, 51, 52, 53, 55, 56, 63, 65, 69, 71, 82, 83, 89, 91, 93, 96, 101, 114
David, King 3
Davidic Covenant .. 3, 17, 31, 34, 47, 55, 83, 114

Dead Sea Scrolls..................................40
Death....8, 9, 10, 17, 26, 34, 36, 38, 39, 67, 68, 91
Deportation..................................88, 107
Deportations...................................88
Derelict..................................22, 36, 105
Destruction of Jerusalem...................9, 91
Devotion..................................20, 52
Discipline..................................37, 89
Discouragement..................................36, 72
Disunity..................................22, 29
Division..................................7, 8, 67, 69, 72, 115
Doubt..................................16, 52, 69, 93, 96
Doxological evangelism.....................28
Doxology..................................52
Duplicate names..................................32
Edom..................................26, 68
Egypt..................................8, 9, 38, 42, 67, 91
Elah..................................67
Elijah..................................8, 67, 68
Elisha..................................8, 67, 68
Encouragement...11, 15, 16, 21, 36, 49, 66, 82, 99, 100, 104, 110
Enemies...11, 13, 22, 26, 28, 37, 38, 84, 96, 110
Enjoying..................................29
Envy..................................42
Epaphroditus..................................22
Ephraim..................................20, 93
Ephraimites..................................86
Esv..................................2, 37, 45, 71, 83, 93, 113
Evangelical..................................3, 10
Evangelism..................................28
Evangelist..................................75, 79, 80
Evangelistic..................................28, 76, 95, 105
Exile..................................7, 9, 10, 11, 16, 93, 107, 108
Exiles...9, 10, 13, 14, 16, 19, 25, 26, 28, 36, 38, 47, 51, 52, 60, 63, 64, 66, 71, 72, 93, 99, 100, 104, 107, 110
Ezra..................................7, 8, 11, 16, 63, 66, 107, 115
Faith....22, 36, 37, 40, 42, 46, 52, 76, 96
Fall of Israel..................................8, 68, 91
Fall of Jerusalem..................................8, 9
Family devotions..................................29
Family tree..................................80, 83, 108, 111
Father....26, 37, 40, 41, 51, 55, 72, 77, 78, 79, 93, 96, 100, 101
Feast..................................17, 21
Feast of Tabernacles..................................17
Federal headship..................................89
Fedora..................................2

Finishing well..................................51
Foreigners..................................68, 88, 93
Forgiveness..................................72, 100
Former Prophets..................................115
Gad..................................8, 17, 20, 88
Gatekeepers..................................17
Genealogy.....7, 8, 12, 13, 15, 16, 17, 19
Genesis 3:11,21..................................88
Gentiles..................................45, 46
Geography..................................14, 16, 113, 114
George Santyana..................................107
Gerome, J.L...................................62
Giant..................................37
Giants..................................37, 38
Gibeon..................................17, 28, 29, 43, 55, 63
Gold..................................7, 60
Good example..................................89, 96
Gospel..................................22, 29, 39
Grace..................................11, 29, 88, 97
Grandmother..................................75
Grandson..................................3, 36, 76
Greek..................................7
Hagiography..................................10
Hanani..................................67, 80
Hanun son of Nahash..................................36
Hazael..................................68, 82
Heart....9, 10, 22, 27, 34, 39, 51, 52, 53, 56, 72, 83, 96, 101, 110, 114
Hebrew..................................7, 40, 110, 115
Hebrew Bible..................................7, 31, 115
Hebron..................................17, 19, 22
Heritage..................................10, 63
Hezekiah..................................8, 47, 91, 93, 95, 96, 98
Hezron..................................12
Hilkiah the high priest..................................106
Hiram..................................26, 57
History..................................8, 10, 52, 114
Holy Spirit..................................34, 96, 101
Homework..................................50, 66, 76, 80
HONESTY..................................52
Hoshea..................................68, 115
House....17, 32, 40, 41, 43, 56, 59, 60, 72, 106, 111
Huldah..................................91, 104
Huldah the prophetess..................................91
HUMILITY..................................52, 56
Humour..................................3, 78
Iddo..................................48, 67
Iddo the seer..................................48
Identity..................................9, 10, 11, 13, 16, 62

Idolatry..................................7, 9, 10, 68, 70, 72, 76
In Christ, being..................................16, 29, 52, 58, 89, 96
Inheritance..................................52, 114
Injustice..................................40
Irony..................................77, 108
Isaiah..................................8, 48, 56, 68, 91, 98, 114, 115
Ish-bosheth..................................17
Israel....7, 8, 10, 11, 12, 17, 19, 21, 23, 26, 32, 39, 42, 45, 47, 48, 55, 67, 68, 69, 70, 74, 76, 77, 83, 86, 88, 91, 93, 100
J(eh)oram..................................8, 68
Jabez..................................15, 16
Jacob..................................12
Jehoahaz..................................8, 68, 91, 108
Jehoash..................................68
Jehoiachin..................................8, 91, 108
Jehoiada..................................68, 83
Jehoiakim..................................8, 91, 108
Jehoram..................................68, 69, 81, 85
Jehoshaphat....8, 67, 77, 78, 79, 80, 81, 85, 89
Jehu..................................67, 68, 82
Jeremiah..................................8, 38, 48, 69, 91, 107, 115
Jeroboam I..................................8, 67, 70, 74, 75, 76
Jeroboam II..................................68
Jesse..................................12, 53
Jewish..................................7, 16, 46, 98
Jews..................................49, 61
Jezebel..................................105
Joab..................................17, 37, 42
Joash..................................68, 83, 85
Joash54..................................83
John Knox..................................101
John Newton..................................97
John the baptist..................................49
Jonah..................................8, 65, 68, 115
Jonathan..................................17
Joram..................................69, 82
Jordan..................................15
Josephus..................................107
Josiah..................................8, 91, 103, 104, 105, 106, 108
Jotham..................................8, 68, 85, 87
Joy..................................21, 26, 52, 63, 89, 96
Judah....7, 8, 14, 17, 19, 22, 39, 48, 51, 55, 67, 68, 69, 70, 74, 75, 76, 77, 83, 86, 88, 89, 91, 93, 95, 97, 107, 108
Judges..................................12, 13, 31, 48, 71, 115
Ketuvim, Writings..................................115
Kireath-Jearim..................................23
Lachish..................................95

General Index

Latter Prophets.................................115
Law..............2, 3, 9, 13, 91, 98, 105, 115
Levites.............17, 25, 26, 31, 47, 48, 49
Leviticus 13-14....................................87
Libnah..68
Line of succession..............................51
Love...............................26, 53, 80, 96
Maacah...76
Manasseh..8, 15, 20, 88, 91, 97, 98, 99, 100, 101, 103, 104, 105
Map...15, 19, 23, 28, 36, 55, 56, 64, 73, 81, 82, 94, 95, 103, 113, 114
Medo-Persian.......................7, 8, 91, 107
Meetings..28, 29
Membership..................3, 21, 42, 48, 80
Menahem..68
Mephibosheth................................17, 36
Mercy..40
Messiah......................9, 11, 38, 66, 110
Messianic king 35, 36, 38, 47, 51, 55, 65, 69, 91
Micaiah..................................8, 67, 78
Michal..17, 27
Mighty men....................................17, 20
Moab..67, 68
Modernistic...10
Moral...13, 14
Moriah, Mount.....................................41
Moses.........................12, 13, 47, 115
Motherhood.....71, 72, 75, 80, 82, 93, 96
Naaman...68
Naboth..67
Nadab...67
Nahshon...12
Nathan..............8, 17, 31, 32, 33, 48, 101
Nations............................9, 26, 45, 79
Neco, Pharaoh..................................108
Nevi'im, Prophets..............................115
New covenant...............................34, 49
NIMSHI...82
NIV......................2, 9, 37, 45, 69, 71, 83
Northern kingdom....7, 9, 69, 70, 74, 87, 88, 93, 99
Nunc dimittis................................38, 45
Obadiah.......................................67, 115
Obed..12
Obed-Edom..26
Obedience..........26, 36, 37, 52, 101, 104
Oded...67, 68
Ofsted..85

Old Covenant...............................31, 47
Old Testament....................................25
Omission..10
Omri..67, 83
Ornan...41
Pagan...9, 99
Paganism.................85, 88, 96, 105, 110
Palace..17
Parable of the tenants.....................109
Passover......................................63, 91
Paton, John..22
Paul..53, 57
Peace.............................43, 45, 46, 89
Pekah..8, 68
Pekahiah..68
Pentateuch..48
Pentecost...34
People of God............................110, 111
Perez..12, 24
Perseverance....................................72
Peter....34, 45, 46, 49, 84, 100, 101, 111
Pharaoh.............................17, 105, 108
Philistia...68
Philistines........................17, 23, 26, 38
Phones..29
Pisidian Antioch.................................53
Post-Christian age..........................110
Post-exilic..10
Praise...17, 52
Prayer 17, 21, 28, 33, 34, 36, 41, 52, 55, 56, 57, 61, 72, 76, 96, 100, 101, 114
Presence..........11, 23, 26, 29, 60, 63, 110
PRIDE.....................................52, 91, 101
Priest..............16, 17, 28, 49, 50, 91, 105
Prodigals..100
Promise.....11, 34, 44, 52, 61, 69, 72, 83
Promises. 16, 33, 34, 36, 60, 63, 72, 82, 83, 84
Public domain.....................................2
Purpose..........................7, 9, 11, 59
Queen of Sheba.....................17, 64, 65
Quiet time..96
Quiet times..29
Ram...12
Ransom..39, 41
Rape..36
Readership..9
Rebuke..36
Regeneration.....................................96
Rehoboam.............8, 67, 69, 70, 71, 72

Reigns..10, 69
Relevance..9
Relevant................10, 14, 16, 47, 107
Remnant...8, 91
Repent...34, 72, 89
REPENTANCE......52, 72, 77, 89, 91, 96
Rephaim...37
Rephaites.....................................37, 38
Risk...20, 21, 22
Rôles..............25, 26, 47, 48, 49, 71, 93
Roll, of members.................................3
Roman Empire..........................113, 114
Rôtas...48
Rules..25
Sabbaths..111
Sacrifice......................9, 13, 17, 42, 66
Samaria....................67, 68, 69, 88, 93
Samaritan..49
Samaritans...................................68, 93
Samuel....3, 8, 9, 10, 12, 14, 17, 24, 25, 27, 31, 36, 37, 39, 42, 48, 71, 115
Sargon II...94
Satan..39, 42
Saul 8, 10, 12, 13, 17, 19, 20, 23, 27, 36, 53
Scholarship..10
Scrolls......................7, 31, 40, 115
Seal...55, 63, 95
Secular age......................................110
Security...47
Sennacherib..........................91, 95, 96
Septuagint...40
Services.................................25, 29, 46
Shallum..68
Shalmaneser V............................88, 94
Shalom..43
Shaphan the secretary....................106
Shechem.....................................12, 13
Sheep...40, 41
Shemaiah......................................48, 67
Shemaiah the prophet......................48
Shepherd..................9, 21, 23, 32, 40
Sheshbazzar....................................107
Shishak..67
Shunammite......................................68
Siege of Samaria..............................68
Sign..55, 63
Simeon..38, 45
Singers..17
Small group......................................29

Small Groups 3
Solomon 8, 9, 10, 11, 17, 19, 29, 31, 41, 43, 44, 45, 46, 47, 48, 51, 52, 53, 55, 56, 57, 59, 63, 64, 65, 66, 69, 70, 72
Son of David 45, 69, 89, 114
Source documents 48
Southern kingdom 7, 9, 69, 70, 74
Sovereignty 16
Spiritual degeneration 70
Sproul, R.C. 25
Syria 68, 76, 113
Syria-Palestina 113
Syrians 17, 42, 78
Tabernacle 29, 32, 43, 47, 63
Talmud 98
Tamar 17, 36
Tanak 31, 115
Temple 7, 8, 9, 13, 17, 25, 29, 31, 32, 36, 38, 41, 42, 43, 44, 45, 46, 47, 48, 51, 53, 55, 56, 59, 60, 61, 62, 63, 64, 66, 68, 83, 91, 96, 105, 106, 110, 111
Temptation 42
Tent 29, 43, 62
Thanksgiving 17, 52
Theology 40
Thirty 17
Tibni 67
Tiglath-Pileser III 88, 94
Tishbe 81
Torah 115
Transjordan 15
Trials 37
Tribe 7, 9, 13, 14, 15, 16, 17, 20, 21, 51, 70, 88, 91
Tribes 7, 9, 13, 15, 16, 17, 20, 21, 70, 88, 91
Twelve tribes, the 70
Type 56
Typology .. 45, 56, 65, 66, 69, 89, 96, 107
Tyre 26, 57
Unfaithfulness 9
Unity 19, 24, 26, 45
Unrepentance 88, 89
Uzzah 10, 17, 24, 25, 26, 39
Uzziah 68, 85, 86
Victim 16
Victory 35, 37, 38, 96
Wailing wall 61
Wallet 52
Warrior 20, 22
Wealth 17, 66, 91
Westminster Confession of Faith 42
Whitewashing 10, 14, 40, 72, 96
Wikimedia Commons 2
Wikipedia 2
Wilberforce, William 22
Winston Churchill 74
Wisdom 8, 10, 11, 17, 45, 55, 57, 70
Witness-bearing 80, 96
Worries 29
Worship ... 16, 17, 27, 28, 29, 42, 46, 47, 52, 60, 63, 72, 91, 96, 111
Yemen 64
Zedekiah 8, 91, 108, 109
Zerubbabel 107
Ziklag 17, 20, 22
Zimri 67
Zion 16
 Judges 12

Scripture Index

Genesis..................p13
Genesis 1:1..................p13
Genesis 5,10,11,35,36..........p12
Genesis 11..................p19
Genesis 22:2..................p59
Genesis 27:29..................p43
Genesis 29:30..................p70
Genesis 37:4..................p71
Genesis 49:10..............pp12,51
Genesis 50:20..........pp13,39,42
Exodus
.....pp3,23,31,32,39,47,83,115
Exodus 2:1-10..................p83
Exodus 25-30..................p47
Exodus 29:45..................p23
Exodus 30:12,16..................p39
Exodus 40:38..................p32
Leviticus..................pp47,49
Leviticus 1:4..................p55
Leviticus 18:28..................p9
Numbers
........pp12,24,31,36,47,76,115
Numbers 4..................p47
Numbers 4:5-6; 15; 17-20; 7:6-9
..................p24
Numbers 4:18-19a..................p24
Numbers 24:17..................p12
Numbers 24:18..................p36
Numbers 27:21..................p24
Numbers 32:23..................p76
Deuteronomy 17:14-17..........p12
Deuteronomy 17:17..............p71
Deuteronomy 17:18......pp26,106
Deuteronomy 18:21..............p33
Deuteronomy 28:15-68............p9
Deuteronomy 29:18..............p84
Deuteronomy 30:11-14........p104
Deuteronomy 33:8-10............p26
Joshua 7:25..................p14
Judges 2:19..................p71
Judges 9..................p12
Judges 21:25..................p13
Ruth..............pp12,19,31,48,115
Ruth 4..................p19
Ruth 4:18-22a..................p12
Samuel............pp7,8,9,10,13,27
1 Samuel 6:19..................p23
1 Samuel 8..................p12
1 Samuel 16:7..................p9
1 Samuel 31:1– 2 Samuel 1:16
..................p8
2 Samuel 1:17–24:1–25..........p8
2 Samuel 6:2..................p24
2 Samuel 6:8..................p10
2 Samuel 10..................p37
2 Samuel 11:2-5..................p71
2 Samuel 11:21..................p12
2 Samuel 13:32-39..............p14
2 Samuel 24:1..................p42
Kings
....
pp7,8,9,10,13,17,31,44,48,65, 66,67,68,70,71,72,81,91,93,9 9,107,108,115
1 Kings 1:1–2:46..................p8
1 Kings 3:1-22:53..................p8
1 Kings 5:3..................p44
1 Kings 11..................pp65,66,72
1 Kings 11:3..................pp10,71
1 Kings 11:4..................p72
1 Kings 11:29-33..................p70
1 Kings 17:1..................p81
1 Kings 22:51-53..................p71
2 Kings..................pp69,99,107
2 Kings 1:1-25:30..................p8
2 Kings 3:1,6..................p69
2 Kings 17..................p9
2 Kings 17:24-41............pp88,93
2 Kings 21:10-18..................p99
2 Kings 25:11..................p9
2 Kings 25:26..................p9
Chronicles

....
pp7,8,9,11,13,16,69,99,114,11 5
1 Chronicles..................pp7,21,56
1 Chronicles 1..................p8
1 Chronicles 1:1-4..................p13
1 Chronicles 1:1–9:44..................p8
1 Chronicles 1:1..............pp13,16
1 Chronicles 1:35-54..............p14
1 Chronicles 2:1..................p15
1 Chronicles 2:1-4..................p14
1 Chronicles 2:3..................p14
1 Chronicles 2:3,4,7..............p14
1 Chronicles 2:3a..................p14
1 Chronicles 2:3-4..................p10
1 Chronicles 2:7..................p14
1 Chronicles 2:13-15..............p14
1 Chronicles 3:1-9..................p14

1 Chronicles 3:4..............pp14,19	1 Chronicles 13......................p39	1 Chronicles 29:17.................p53
1 Chronicles 3:9....................p14	1 Chronicles 13:3............pp23,24	1 Chronicles 29:19.................p53
1 Chronicles 3:17..................p14	1 Chronicles 13:6..................p24	1 Chronicles 29:21-29:30........p8
1 Chronicles 4:9....................p16	1 Chronicles 13:7-10.............p39	1 Chronicles 29:23.................p19
1 Chronicles 4:9-10...............p15	1 Chronicles 13:12................p25	1 Chronicles 29:25.................p10
1 Chronicles 4:10..................p16	1 Chronicles 13:14................p26	2 Chronicles....................pp7,56
1 Chronicles 5:1-2.................p14	1 Chronicles 14:1-2...............p26	2 Chronicles 1.......................p45
1 Chronicles 5:1..............pp10,14	1 Chronicles 14:2..................p26	2 Chronicles 1:1–21:3..............p8
1 Chronicles 5:18-22.............p15	1 Chronicles 14:3..................p10	2 Chronicles 1:1....................p55
1 Chronicles 5:20..................p16	1 Chronicles 14:8-17.............p26	2 Chronicles 2:11..................p57
1 Chronicles 5:22..................p16	1 Chronicles 15...............pp25,27	2 Chronicles 3:1....................p41
1 Chronicles 5:26..................p14	1 Chronicles 15:29................p27	2 Chronicles 5:2-14...............p63
1 Chronicles 6:15..................p14	1 Chronicles 16:8-36.............p27	2 Chronicles 5:2....................p60
1 Chronicles 8:29-38.............p19	1 Chronicles 17:4-14.............p34	2 Chronicles 5:7....................p60
1 Chronicles 9......................p16	1 Chronicles 17:8-11..............p11	2 Chronicles 5:10..................p60
1 Chronicles 9:1-3..................p15	1 Chronicles 17:11-13............p33	2 Chronicles 6......................p60
1 Chronicles 9:1-34...............p13	1 Chronicles 17:12-14............p44	2 Chronicles 6:16..................p69
1 Chronicles 9:1....................p16	1 Chronicles 17:14..........pp33,34	2 Chronicles 7:16..................p72
1 Chronicles 9:1,3.................p51	1 Chronicles 17:15................p32	2 Chronicles 9......................p45
1 Chronicles 9:3....................p16	1 Chronicles 18:14................p19	2 Chronicles 9:22-23.............p11
1 Chronicles 9:35-44.............p13	1 Chronicles 19...............pp36,37	2 Chronicles 9:30..................p19
1 Chronicles 10....................p19	1 Chronicles 19:13................p37	2 Chronicles 10:15.................p72
1 Chronicles 10:1–14...............p8	1 Chronicles 19:16................p37	2 Chronicles 10:16.................p19
1 Chronicles 10:13-14...........p19	1 Chronicles 20:4,6,8.............p37	2 Chronicles 11:2-4...............p70
1 Chronicles 11:1,10..............p19	1 Chronicles 21:1..................p42	2 Chronicles 11:4..................p72
1 Chronicles 11:1..................p19	1 Chronicles 21:2..................p42	2 Chronicles 11:16................p70
1 Chronicles 11:1-29:20...........p8	1 Chronicles 21:8..................p10	2 Chronicles 12:14................p72
1 Chronicles 11:2..................p21	1 Chronicles 21:13................p40	2 Chronicles 13:10-12............p75
1 Chronicles 11:5..................p19	1 Chronicles 21:14................p40	2 Chronicles 13:10-20............p76
1 Chronicles 11:18-19............p20	1 Chronicles 21:17..........pp40,41	2 Chronicles 14:6..................p75
1 Chronicles 11:18................p20	1 Chronicles 21:23................p41	2 Chronicles 15:2..................p76
1 Chronicles 12....................p21	1 Chronicles 21:25-22:1.........p59	2 Chronicles 15:8-9...............p76
1 Chronicles 12:1..................p20	1 Chronicles 21:26................p42	2 Chronicles 15:8..................p76
1 Chronicles 12:2..................p20	1 Chronicles 21:30................p40	2 Chronicles 15:16................p76
1 Chronicles 12:8,16.............p20	1 Chronicles 22:1..................p41	2 Chronicles 16:1-2...............p76
1 Chronicles 12:14................p20	1 Chronicles 22:8..................p10	2 Chronicles 16:7-9...............p78
1 Chronicles 12:19................p20	1 Chronicles 23:26................p47	2 Chronicles 16:14................p75
1 Chronicles 12:23-37...........p21	1 Chronicles 27:24................p48	2 Chronicles 17-21................p76
1 Chronicles 12:30................p20	1 Chronicles 27:25ff...............p48	2 Chronicles 17:3..................p77
1 Chronicles 12:38................p21	1 Chronicles 28....................p42	2 Chronicles 17:8-9...............p26
1 Chronicles 12:39-40...........p21	1 Chronicles 28:8..................p52	2 Chronicles 17:11.................p81
1 Chronicles 12:40................p21	1 Chronicles 28:12................p47	2 Chronicles 18:13-16............p78

Scripture Index

2 Chronicles 18:26..................p78	Psalm 49:7-9.........................p41	Matthew 28:18-20................p66
2 Chronicles 18:33........pp78,105	Psalm 72........................pp20,66	Mark 1:11...............................p44
2 Chronicles 19:2....................p80	Psalm 72:14b........................p20	Mark 1:15.............................p107
2 Chronicles 20:29..................p79	Psalm 96................................p27	Mark 4:1-20...........................p84
2 Chronicles 20:31..................p80	Psalm 105..............................p27	Luke 1:32-33..........................p44
2 Chronicles 20:32..................p80	Psalm 106..............................p27	Luke 2:27-32..........................p45
2 Chronicles 21:4–36:21...........p8	Psalm 116:16.........................p71	Luke 2:28-32..........................p45
2 Chronicles 24:1....................p83	Isaiah 11:3............................p114	Luke 2:30................................p38
2 Chronicles 24:17-18.............p83	Isaiah 37:38...........................p96	Luke 2:36................................p16
2 Chronicles 26:15-19..........p109	Jeremiah 25:11....................p107	Luke 10:32..............................p49
2 Chronicles 28:22..................p88	Jeremiah 25:12; 29:10............p7	Luke 11:29-32........................p65
2 Chronicles 29:3-27...............p93	Jeremiah 33:17......................p69	Luke 11:30..............................p65
2 Chronicles 30:6-9.................p95	Jeremiah 39-45....................p107	Luke 11:31..............................p65
2 Chronicles 32.......................p96	Jeremiah 47:1-4.....................p38	Luke 11:32..............................p65
2 Chronicles 32:1....................p95	Lamentations...............pp48,115	Luke 13:34-35........................p52
2 Chronicles 32:8....................p95	Ezekiel 25:10..........................p37	Luke 15...................................p99
2 Chronicles 32:10-15.............p95	Daniel 9:2...............................p64	Luke 17:20............................p113
2 Chronicles 32:24-26.............p96	Jonah 1:3................................p65	Luke 18:38............................p114
2 Chronicles 33.....................p100	Haggai....................................p13	Luke 20:41-44........................p96
2 Chronicles 33:23......pp103,104	Haggai 1:1..............................p66	Luke 22:20..............................p34
2 Chronicles 34:22................p105	Zechariah.....pp13,48,66,68,115	Luke 24:27..............................p65
2 Chronicles 35:3.............pp47,66	Zechariah 4:10.......................p66	John 1:19................................p49
2 Chronicles 36:15-21..........p107	Matthew 1..............................p41	John 2:19-21..........................p45
2 Chronicles 36:15-19..........p109	Matthew 1:1...........................p69	John 4:22................................p93
2 Chronicles 36:22–23.............p8	Matthew 1:21.........................p41	John 13:35..............................p19
2 Chronicles 36:22-23............p14	Matthew 4:13.........................p16	John 14:16-18........................p66
Ezra....................pp8,11,13,22	Matthew 5:5...........................p52	John 14:23..............................p26
Ezra 1:1-4...............................p8	Matthew 6:10.......................p114	John 15:7................................p55
Ezra 1:8-11............................p13	Matthew 6:21.........................p53	John 17:20-23........................p19
Ezra 1:8................................p107	Matthew 6:33.........pp56,110,111	John 18:7-8............................p41
Ezra 2:61-63..........................p16	Matthew 8:20.........................p43	Acts 1:8................................p114
Ezra 3:12................................p63	Matthew 12:6.........................p66	Acts 2:38-39..........................p34
Ezra 4:1..................................p11	Matthew 12:20.......................p38	Acts 4:11................................p45
Ezra 6:15................................p64	Matthew 12:28.....................p114	Acts 4:36................................p49
Ezra 6:17................................p64	Matthew 12:33.....................p100	Acts 10:36..............................p46
Ezra 6:19-22..........................p63	Matthew 13:15.......................p53	Acts 13:22.......................pp53,83
Ezra 9:6..................................p11	Matthew 15:18.......................p53	Romans 1:7; 5:1; 16:20.........p46
Nehemiah...............................p22	Matthew 16:18.......................p45	Romans 2:4............................p72
Nehemiah 2:19.......................p22	Matthew 21:33-45................p109	Romans 3:23..........................p40
Nehemiah 8:8..........................p9	Matthew 21:41-43................p109	Romans 4:13..........................p52
Psalms...............pp3,7,27,48,115	Matthew 22:37.......................p53	Romans 6:23..........................p40
Psalm 34:8.............................p65	Matthew 26:28.......................p40	Romans 8:1.....................pp84,89

Romans 8:15-17 .... p84	Philippians 1:2; 4:7 .... p46	Hebrews 13:12 .... p59
Romans 8:28 .... pp39,42	Philippians 2:25,29-30 .... p20	Hebrews 13:20-21 .... p46
Romans 14:17 .... p114	Philippians 3:17 .... p22	James 1:5 .... p57
Romans 15 .... p45	Philippians 3:20 .... p66	James 1:13-15 .... p39
Romans 15:2 .... p45	Philippians 4:4-6 .... p27	James 4:2 .... p58
Romans 16:3-4 .... p20	Colossians 1:9 .... p57	1 Peter 1:2 .... p46
1 Corinthians 1:3 .... p46	1 Thessalonians 1:1; 5:23 ..... p46	1 Peter 2:1-12 .... p49
1 Corinthians 3:10 .... p29	1 Thessalonians 4:16-18 .... p66	1 Peter 2:5 .... p45
1 Corinthians 3:16 .... p61	1 Thessalonians 5:16-18 .... p96	1 Peter 5:5-6 .... p100
1 Corinthians 10:11 .... p66	2 Thessalonians 1:2 .... p46	2 Peter 1:2 .... p46
1 Corinthians 13:1-7 .... p53	2 Thessalonians 3:3 .... p11	2 Peter 1:10 .... p84
1 Corinthians 13:4-7 .... p53	1 Timothy 1:2 .... p46	2 Peter 3:11-12 .... p111
1 Corinthians 15:55 .... p38	1 Timothy 5:17 .... p26	1 John 5:13-17 .... p84
1 Corinthians 15:57 .... p38	2 Timothy 1:2 .... p46	2 John 3 .... p46
2 Corinthians 1:2 .... p46	Titus 1:4 .... p46	Jude 20-23 .... p84
2 Corinthians 3:14 .... p47	Titus 1:7 .... p14	Revelation p114
2 Corinthians 5:21 .... p41	Philemon 3 .... p46	Revelation 3:5 .... p89
Galatians 1:3 .... p46	Hebrews 1:5 .... p44	Revelation 3:7 .... p26
Galatians 4:6 .... p53	Hebrews 1:8 .... p44	Revelation 7 .... p21
Ephesians pp3,89	Hebrews 10:23-25 .... p84	Revelation 7:9-17 .... p21
Ephesians 1:2 .... p46	Hebrews 10:25 .... p9	Revelation 7:9-14 .... p89
Ephesians 2:21 .... p62	Hebrews 12:5-6 .... p89	Revelation 20:13 .... p89
Ephesians 3:20 .... p58	Hebrews 12:7 .... p37	Revelation 21:1 .... p114
Ephesians 4:11-12 .... p45	Hebrews 12:11-15 .... p84	Revelation 21:22 .... p62
Ephesians 4:12 .... p45	Hebrews 12:22 .... p16	Revelation 22:16 .... p114
Philippians. .pp20,22,27,46,57,66	Hebrews 13:10-13 .... p62	

Please see the table of **Contents** starting on page 5.

Please check the **General Index** (page 117) for subjects without obvious headings in the above table of contents.

The **Scripture Index** (page 121) allows you to work backwards from Bible texts to their use in this manual.

Also available on Amazon and other sellers:

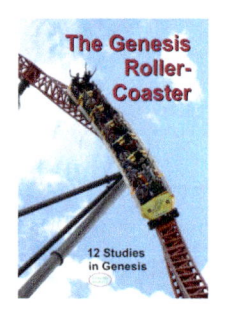

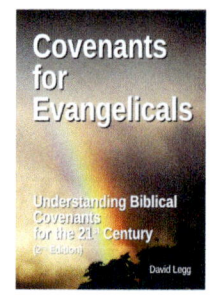

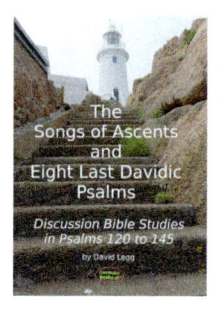

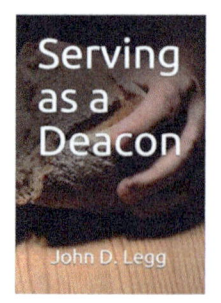

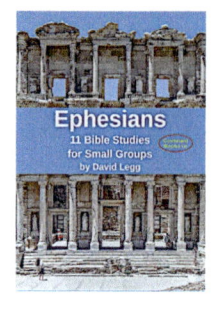

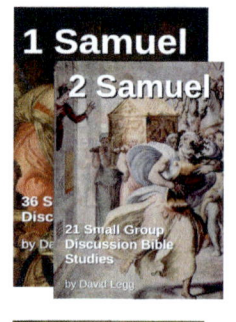

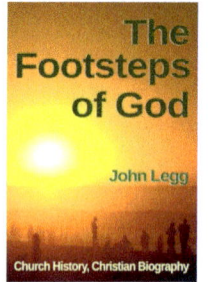

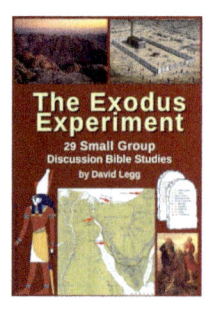

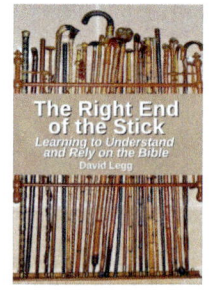

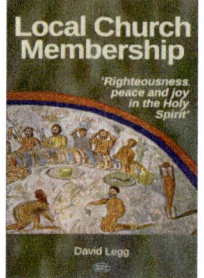

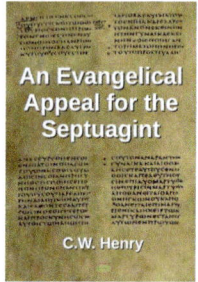

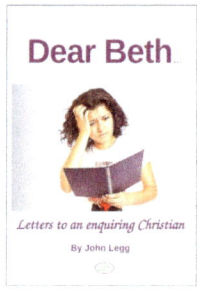

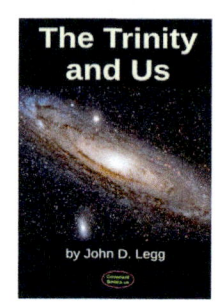

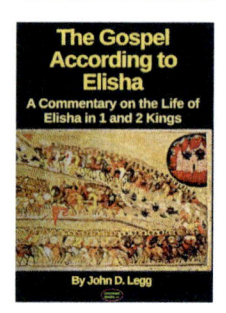

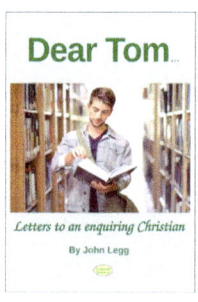

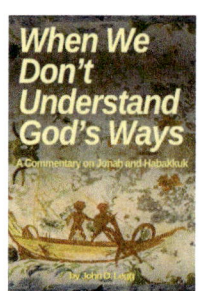

Printed in Great Britain
by Amazon